Pourin' Down Rain

by Cheryl Foggo

Detselig Enterprises
Calgary, Alberta

©1990 Cheryl Foggo

Canadian Cataloguing in Publication Data
Foggo, Cheryl
Pourin' down rain

ISBN 1-55059-010-3
1. Foggo, Cheryl.   2. Foggo family.
3. Black Canadians--Alberta--Biography.
I. Title.
FC3700.B6F63 1990   971.23'00496
F1080.N3F63 1990   C90-091280-4

Detselig Enterprises Ltd.
P.O. Box G 399
Calgary, Alberta T3A 2G3

Printed in Canada
SAN 115-0324
ISBN 1-55059-010-3

Dedication

*For my Brother, Ronny, who died November 28, 1985,
without having the opportunity
to know my children;
for Noël's little Josie
and
David L. Smith*

Acknowledgments

I would like to acknowledge the assistance of the following people and organizations:

First and especially, Daisy Williams
Ellis Smith
Bert and Edith Smith
Sidney and Eileen Smith
Olie and Cathy Smith
David and Barbara Smith
Ethel and Lawrence Lewsey
Edith and Andrew Risby
Pearl and Allen Hayes
Pauline and Roy Foggo
Eva Goodman
Clem Martini
Jill Swartz
Penny Williams
Fil Fraser
David Bercuson
Jon Whyte
Larry Pratt
Howard and Tamara Palmer

The Canada Council
The Alberta Foundation for the Literary Arts
Alberta Culture and Multiculturalism

Table of Contents

Introduction

$\mathcal{U}$pon occasion when I was growing up, we went to eat in Chinatown.

Sometimes the occasion was a visit from an out-of-town relation; sometimes the occasion was unknown to me, perhaps unknown to everyone except Aunt Edie and Uncle Andrew, who acted as co-chairs for these Chinatown excursions. All of my family — my mother, father, sister and brothers; all of our aunts and uncles, cousins and many people who I thought were my aunts, uncles and cousins and a few people who were not Black at all, but were so much a part of my world that I thought they were Black in a different way — all of us went to Chinatown.

We were stared at, of course. In 1965 it was rare to see a large group of mostly Black people in Calgary. I believed that the staring was something we had earned, an acknowledgement of our status as important and beautiful people.

The women wore hats, the men wore long coats and rubber, slip-on covers for their shoes. Some faces were dark and shiny, others were light brown and waxy looking. The teenage boy cousins wore stove-pipe pants and had very lean faces, the girls wore white lipstick over textured mouths. I was in love with these people who were a magnet to the eyes of all who passed them. I loved to hear them laugh and see them point to the menu, saying, "I'd like to try some of this here," or "The onliest thing about Chinese food is you git hungry again later."

This book is for all of them — the aunts, uncles, cousins, sisters, brothers, the friends who I believed to be Black in their own way, and for those who stared at us in Chinatown and wondered what we were doing there — this is so you will know.

Meeting Jim Crow

. . skin is a badge that you will always wear, a form of identification for those in the world who wish to brand you . . .

There was nothing amiss, nothing lacking in Bowness. In 1958, my parents bought a house there for seven thousand dollars. It had no plumbing, no basement, no porch, an unfinished yard and only five small rooms.

Our street, 70th Street, was gravel and dust. No street lamps. No trees. When the wind blew, which it did frequently, great clouds of sand would whirl up and spin across the road. My brothers and sister and I, and our friends, were delighted by these dust storms. Someone would shriek, "It's a tornado!" and we would chase the cloud, madly laughing.

Around the corner and up 46th Avenue was a cluster of businesses — the bakery, the hardware store, Gibson's Variety, a cafe, the library and the Crystal Grocery, which everyone referred to as "Garry's," after the proprietor, Garry Fong.

At the other end of 70th Street was Bowcroft Elementary which my brothers attended, and the kindergarten which I attended in the basement of the United Church. Before gaining the church doors, there was a long, wide, grassy field to master. Initially, the crossing of this field required a certain amount of courage-gathering. The grass was, in places, as tall as I and the boulders in the distance might have provided cover for an animal or a bully. Soon, though, bolstered by the company of my friend Ricky Hayes, the field's gently waving rainbow-colored foxtails became a treasured part of the enjoyment in a five-year-old life.

Richard's Birthday, May 1962.

Our street contained the closest thing to a Black community that one would find in Calgary in 1961. Ricky Hayes' parents were biracial, but he, his brother Randy and sister Debbie considered themselves Black. The Hayes', their grandparents across the alley, my family and the Saunders and Lawson families up the road comprised what I believe was the largest concentration of Black people in a single Calgary neighborhood.

My parents had an attitude of kinship toward the other Black families on the street. The families knew one another, they knew each other's parents and grandparents, and probably because of that "knowing," they communicated to us our connection to other Black children. We played together. Without isolating ourselves from the other children in the neighborhood and without any discussion of it, we sensed a link that transcended our environs.

Across the street from our house was another field which we had to cross to reach the railroad tracks leading to the twin bridges, the Bow River, and ultimately, to the paths that took us "up in the hills."

Most summer days we spent meandering along the tracks to the river, the usual goal being a picnic in the hills. The picnic, however, was not really the point. The point was the adventure we would sometimes encounter along the way.

On a very warm day, if there was no breeze, the heat from the iron rails and sharp smell of oil and metal bouncing up into our faces would drive us down from the tracks to walk through the high grasses. This meant slower going, but it was good to sniff the flowers instead of the heat and to dig around what someone would insist was a badger hole.

From the first time my brothers pronounced me old enough to go along with them, until I was sixteen and we moved from Bowness, the journey along the tracks to the river, across the bridges and up into the hills was real life. It was the meeting place, it was where we went to talk and light campfires, it was something we did that our parents did not do.

Across the alley from us lived two children, a brother and sister, who never joined the treks to the hills if we and the Hayes children were going. Their father forbade them from associating with us, and effectively ostracized his children from the rest of the neighborhood by prohibiting them from joining any games where we Black children were present. When groups formed for kick-the-can or softball, we were often aware of these two children's eyes peering out from the cracks in their fence. They were there, we were aware of their presence, and in retrospect, their loneliness seems palpable.

When I was young, I was minimally aware that racism was a special problem. People who shared our neighbor's prejudices seemed so rare and to have so little effect on my life that I did not attribute their bigotry to a world condition.

My mother had implanted in the minds of my two older brothers, my younger sister and myself that we were special, not ordinary in any way. She would refer to our bigoted neighbor with utter contempt, as "the likes of him," implying that his ideas and his two unfortunate children were unworthy of our time or thoughts.

The diligence of our mother freed the minds of me and my siblings from the self-hatred that can cripple Black children born in ghettos.

Still, even a fiercely proud mother's constant reassurances cannot protect her Black child from learning, sooner or later, that skin is a badge you will always wear, a form of identification for those in the world who wish to brand you.

One afternoon upon returning from school I overheard my mother talking on the telephone to Mr. Leavitt, the principal of my elementary school. He was calling to plead with her to try to persuade Floyd Hayes to discourage his children from fighting at school. Floyd was the brother of my mother's twin sister's husband and the father of the aforementioned friends, Randy, Ricky and Debbie.

"I'm afraid that I can't agree with you, Mr. Leavitt," she was saying. "I'm not going to tell them how to handle their problems. They came from a place where they can't fight. Where they come from a Black person doesn't have a chance against racists, and if Mr. Hayes has decided his children are going to fight name-calling with their fists, that's up to him."

When my mother replaced the receiver on its hook on the wall, I pestered her with questions. What did Mr. Leavitt want? Why had he called her? Were Randy and Ricky in trouble? What did she mean when she said Floyd had come from somewhere else where they couldn't fight it? Fight what?

"Jim Crow. They couldn't fight Jim Crow down there, but he's determined he's going to fight it here."

"Who is Jim Crow?"

"It's not who, it's what. It's called Jim Crow when Black people aren't allowed to ride at the front of the bus, or drink from the same fountains as Whites."

"Jim Crow?" I repeated. "Jim Crow. Where is the Jim Crow?"

"Kansas. Floyd and them were all born in Kansas."

If Floyd "and them" were all born in Kansas, that meant that my Uncle Allen, Floyd's younger brother, had been born there too, and that he had lived with this Jim Crow.

"Is Kansas in Canada?" I asked nervously.

"No, oh no," my mother said. "We don't have that kind of thing here. Kansas is in the States. Allen and Floyd and them never went to the movie houses when they were kids, not because they didn't believe in it, but because nobody was going to tell them that they had to sit up in the balcony or at the back. They came to Canada to get away from that, and they figure they're not going to tell their kids to stand by while anyone calls them 'nigger' either."

My mother was clearly quite agitated by Mr. Leavitt's call. I knew that she would repeat the entire conversation, with some embellishment, to her sisters Pearl and Edie on the telephone later that evening.

As for me, I was relieved to learn that Kansas was not in Canada. Here was yet another story, another horrific tale of life in "The States," fuelling my growing belief that I was lucky to have been born in Canada.

Only short days before Mr. Leavitt's call I had learned that my grandparents, my mother's father and mother, had also once lived in America.

The discovery came to me when I asked my mother to explain why my grandpa was White, yet his brother, Uncle Buster, was Black.

My grandfather was something less than five feet, ten inches tall. He had grey eyes, he wore glasses over his long, narrow nose and he was light-skinned.

He had been called George Washington Smith at birth, but upon joining the Canadian Army in 1919 he revealed the full extent of his embarrassment over the name and lied to his commanding officer, saying that his middle initial stood for Willis. Thereafter, he was known as George Willis Smith and that is how I knew him.

I believe he possessed an average build, although it is difficult to be certain as he always dressed in loose clothing, in particular a pair of grey-biege pants and a yellow shirt.

He had a deep voice and a low, rolling, rumbling laugh. He began most sentences with the phrase, "Well, ya take." He called his five sons "Son," his four daughters "Daughter" and he some-times called me "Granddaughter."

He would say, "Well, ya take, granddaughter, I don't yodel when big girls (referring to my grandmother, who was singing in the kitchen) are listenin'. I only yodel for special small girls."

He was born in Chandler, Oklahoma, on October 31st, 1897. When I say that he was light-skinned, I mean that his skin color was indistinguishable from that of any White person.

That is why, in 1963 when I was seven years old, I asked my mother how he could be White and his brother be Black.

She turned and stared at me. "Your Grandpa is not White."

"He is," I said.

I went to the china cabinet and took the photograph of my grandparents with their children taken on the occasion of their fortieth wedding anniversary. Carefully, I took it to my mother and placed it in her hands

"Look."

My mother took the picture and brushed it gently, wiping away imaginary dust.

"He has very fair skin, honey, but he isn't a White man. What he would say if he knew his grandchildren thought so!" She was very amused and continued, "You see, just look at his hair."

I looked, but seeing nothing remarkable about his metallic-grey, brushed-back hair, did not speak.

"You're not going to find any White man on earth with hair like that," she said. "Daddy has him some bad hair."

"Bad" was how she described any head of hair, like my brother Richard's or my cousin Sharon's, that was very tight and nappy.

Grandparents' fortieth wedding anniversary, August 1959. Seated left to right: Pauline Foggo, Ethel Lewsey, Arrenna Smith, George Smith, Edie Risby, Pearl Hayes. Standing (back row) left to right: Margaret Smith, Eileen Smith, Barbara Smith, Lawrence Lewsey, Bert Smith, Willie Glover, Olie Smith, Sidney Smith, Allen Hayes, Dave Smith, Terry Smith, Willis Smith, Eileen Smith, Elaine Lewsey.

She frequently caused me considerable grief by comparing my hair with my sister's, whose loose and supple hair qualified as "good hair."

I continued to gaze glumly at the photograph in my mother's hand. I was embarrassed at having been wrong about my grandfather. There he sat, beside my dark-skinned grandmother, to whom all along I thought he had been blissfully and interracially married.

"Grandma is Black." I finally said.

"Uhhm hmm, no one would ever mistake your grandmother for White. Daddy and Mama used to run into trouble when they went back to the States. If Daddy wears a hat, you see, he can't lay claim to his heritage. He used to wonder why nobody bothered him when he went into the White areas.

"Once, Mama and Daddy went to Oklahoma to see Mom's relatives. They'd been shopping and made plans to meet in a restaurant for lunch. Daddy got there first, took a table and told the waiter that he was waiting for his wife. He didn't take his hat off until he sat down. When Mama got there she joined Daddy at his table, but no one came to take their order. The waiter walked all around them, just like they weren't there. He acted like he was deaf when Daddy said 'Excuse me.'

"Finally a person came from the kitchen and whispered, 'I'm sorry, but we won't be able to serve you today.'

"Daddy was shocked. He was a young boy when they left the States and had forgotten what it was like there. He really got angry. He stood up and said, 'You sure were planning to serve me before I took my hat off.' He started to go toward the man, but Mama stopped him. 'No George, let's just get our things and go,' she said, 'We don't need for you to land up in jail down here.' Mama and daddy got out of there and shook the dust of that place off of their feet. Daddy's never gone back again, never again."

Knowing my grandparents to be the gentle, lovely people that they were, I couldn't imagine what kind of madness would cause them to be treated in such a manner. I began to fear the very words whenever I heard someone refer to "The States." I vowed that I, like my grandfather, would not bother to darken America's doorstep.

Thinking it over now, it is easy for me to see what would have been the most difficult thing about the Oklahoma experience for my grandfather. To walk away from a man who had insulted his wife by refusing to serve her would have been contrary to his principles. He believed that among his functions, one of his "jobs" was to protect his wife. It was up to him to see that life provided her the ordinary dignities that she deserved.

Following the conversation with my mother that day, I sat down to write my grandparents a letter. I did not mention the story that my mother had told me. I mentioned that I had recently had my tonsils removed, that we would be, as usual, travelling to Winnipeg to see them during the Easter break from school and that I no longer wept when my mother washed my hair.

Hairday

. . . she not only conquered my tears, but Mary's hair as well, pressing it into submission . . .

*H*airday, as my sister and I referred to it, was a torment, a day of relentless brushing, pulling, plunging into the yellow tub of water and then, at the end, the dreaded "hot comb." After a vigorous towel-drying at the hands of our mother, there was an hour's grace for air-drying, then we endured another hour, longer for me because of my thicker (bad) hair, beside the gas stove. We were stationed in a kitchen chair, eye-level with the blue flame that licked and scorched the heavy, iron pressing comb. Our mother divided our hair into tiny strands, coated each strand with Vaseline (wealthier Black people than we ordered products they called "Brilliantine" from the U.S. for this purpose) then applied the teeth of the comb from our scalps to the ends of our hair. We felt the heat, heard the sizzle, smelled the burning protein and saw the smoke rise into the air around us.

As tortuous as hairday was for Noël and I, it must have been triply so for my mother. By the end of the day spent wrestling with our hair and her own, she was always exhausted. Enduring my wailing atop everything else was clearly too much for her. It was a bit of genius on her part to tell me one evening that the next day was hairday, but that my friend Mary would also be coming to spend the day.

Her purpose in dropping both bits of news at the same time was to distract me from the unpleasantness of hairday. She wished to avoid the arguing and the protests that I would normally have presented and at first her ploy worked.

I lay in the bed that I shared with my sister for a long time, pondering my dilemma. If I could think of a reasonable excuse for not having my hair done the next day, how would it affect Mary's visit? Saying that I was already committed to other plans with friends wouldn't do, it would imply that I didn't want Mary to come. I could think of no excuse that would allow for both Mary's visit and my not being available for hair-washing. Also, if I offered too vigorous a protest, might my mother become annoyed with me to the point of threatening to cancel the visit from Mary?

I shared my concerns with my sister. Noël, who was two and a half years younger than I, was equally as opposed to hairday, but due to my status as the elder, it fell to me to conduct negotiations with our mother.

Noël suggested that we tell mom we weren't feeling well.

"No," I said. "She'll just say, 'You'll feel better in the morning' or 'Maybe Mary better come another day.'"

"Yeah. She never listens anyway. We always get hairday, even when it's not fair."

I nodded. "Maybe I'll just tell her that if we have to have our hair done there won't be time to play."

"Okay, say that."

I swung my legs over the edge of the bed and padded out to the kitchen where my mother was ironing.

"Mommy," I said.

She shook her head. "It's late. You kids should be asleep."

"But Mommy, how can we play tomorrow if we have to . . ."

She was about to interrupt me when the phone rang. My heart sank, knowing that it would be one of my aunts, Pearl or Edie, and that I would have no chance to present my case.

"Go to bed," my mother mouthed silently as she took the phone.

I stood in front of her for a short time, but she closed her eyes. "Hi Pearl. Oh nothing. Just ironing."

I marched back to my room and flopped into the bed, snapping the covers over myself.

"Did you tell her?" my sister inquired.

"She wouldn't listen and then Aunt Pearl phoned."

Noël sighed. "They'll be on there for hours."

"I hate hairday," I said.

"Me too."

The results of Hairday! Richard (8), Noel (5), Cheryl (7) and Ronnie (9).

The next morning, just before my mother plunged my head into the yellow tub, she looked at Mary, who was sitting, smiling, in a chair near the door. "I'll bet you don't cry when you get your hair done, do you Mary?" she said.

"No," Mary said, still grinning.

I, of course, shed nary a tear that hairday, nor at any other in the future.

As for my mother, she achieved more than one goal. Added to her victory over my tears, was the opportunity to "do" Mary's hair, a chance that she had clearly been waiting for.

I had once overheard her talking about Mary to one of her sisters. "I don't think Margaret knows what to do with her hair," she had said.

Mary, the accidental product of a biracial liaison, had been adopted into the family of one of my father's post office co-workers, Ray, and his wife Margaret. They were a remarkable couple, both Caucasian, whose mostly adopted family of five included children who are usually hard to place — biracial, handicapped or older children. My mother admired them very much, but often fretted about Mary's hair, which she believed was a puzzle to her adoptive mother. By inviting Mary to visit us on hairday she not only conquered my tears, but Mary's hair as well, pressing it into submission the way that she did to my hair, my sister's and her own.

Willis Augustus

*. . . from those gatherings . . . I learned how to tell a story,
the importance of the family and our history . . .*

True to the promise I had made to my grandparents in the letter, we embarked upon our annual car trip to Winnipeg during the Easter break from school the next spring, 1964.

The drive from Calgary to Winnipeg is a long and tedious one, made longer by the incredibly slow rate of speed my father chose to drive at and the fact that our cars were always very old and drafty. These were minor drawbacks, however. In fact, my brothers, Richard and Ronny, and my sister Noël and I did not come to think of them as drawbacks until we were much older. The trips to Winnipeg were the same as a trip to paradise. We read books, played games and waited in the back seat with varying degrees of patience while our father made semi-frequent stops at the roadside for naps. Very rarely, if there was extra money, we stopped for the night at a motel and considered it a great luxury, regardless of the state of repair or disrepair that it was in. A mental note was made of the presence of a swimming pool, to be later reported to friends at home, minus the detail that it was filled with snowdrifts and dirt rather than water.

We even delighted in stopping for meals in towns like Medicine Hat and Swift Current, although the open-mouthed and unabashed stares that we received would be enough to put me off of my dinner now. Small-town prairie dwellers made no attempt to hide the fact that they had never seen a Black, or for all that we know, a non-White person before. If we were bothered by their gapes and whispers and complained to our mother, she would say, "Don't pay them any attention. They're ignorant."

We would attempt to follow her instructions, except occasionally Richard would stare down or even wave to an inveterate gawker and the rest of us would giggle hysterically behind our hands.

The closer we got to Winnipeg, the more restless we became. The anticipation at seeing our cousins and grandparents was unbearable and our parents tried to hold their frayed nerves in check as they repeated every ten minutes to one of us, "We're almost there. Just around the corner."

When finally we pulled up to 636 Ross Avenue, where our grandparents lived, we exploded out of the car, ignoring our mother's cries of, "Remember, you kids behave!" and pounded up the sidewalk calling out to our grandmother and grandfather that we had arrived.

The house was a smallish bungalow on a quiet street, with a large, bright kitchen that I loved. A doorway from the kitchen led to a spare room where we were allowed to play with our cousins, with no adult shouting, "Be quiet" or "Settle down."

The living room, which was filled with the kind of dark furniture and old things that the elderly gather around them, was a place that I visited at night, because that is where the adults would talk while I sat silently near my mother, eagerly absorbing every word they said, every nuance, every gesture.

It was not unusual, during the sixties, for several of my mother's siblings to be together in their parent's livingroom. Some of them lived in Winnipeg; the others would make plans to travel to that city at the same time. I feel quite certain that for most of them, the highlight of their year began and ended with the vacation that brought them together at 636 Ross Avenue.

I learned a good deal, at an early age from those gatherings. I learned how to tell a story, the importance of the family and our

Family gathering, February 1957. Left to right. Front row: Elaine Lewsey, Cheryl Foggo, Brian Risby, Richard Foggo. Middle row: Dave Smith, Pearl (Smith) Hayes, Olie Smith, Pauline Foggo. Back row: Willis Smith, Edie (Smith) Risby, George Smith, Arrenna Smith, Ethel Lewsey, Lorrie Lewsey, Sidney Smith.

history and I began to learn the way Black people, at least the kind of Black people that we are, use language.

My mother spoke to her family in a way that she never spoke to our neighbors at home. Sometimes she said "ain't" or "don't" when she meant "doesn't," as in, "don't make no difference."

Why, I wondered, would she say "don't make no difference" when I knew quite well that at home she would say "doesn't matter?"

With the exception of Aunt Edie, who had married a man from a rural Black community and adopted some of his expressions and speech patterns, none of Mother's family used expressions like "y'all" as part of their natural speech. One would not have known it, however, from listening to them when they were together in the security of their parents' home. Their high-spirited conversation was heavily peppered with "y'alls" and "uhhm uhhm uhhms" and other colloquialisms usually associated with rural Black American speech.

I began to understand, as I grew older, that they did this to entertain one another and to affirm their "Blackness." They were people with ambivalent feelings about their isolation from other Blacks. They had no desire to return to the America that their parents had fled, nor did they wish to be completely swallowed by the White society in which they all lived.

Their normal speech demonstrated to White society that Black Canadians could speak the Queen's English too.

"Talking Black" to one another, to relatives and to trusted Black friends allowed them to also *feel* Black. It was a method that they used to gain acceptance into the Black communities (small though they were) of Calgary, Vancouver, and Winnipeg when they left Regina. By manipulating their English they could demonstrate to their new Black friends that although they had been raised almost exclusively among Whites, they were still Black inside.

Uncle Willis at the house on Ottawa Street, 1941.

One evening during our 1964 visit, Uncle Willis joined our family and his brothers and sisters at their parents' home. Although he lived in Winnipeg, we did not always see him when we were there. He was a hard drinker and sometimes hard to find.

He had been drinking before his arrival that night and was, therefore, loose and talkative. He wanted to talk about the war, a subject that he broached only when he was intoxicated.

He had, as always, a cigarette with a long ash dangling from his lips and teeth as he spoke and he stopped frequently to cough, his deep, dry, terrible cough that shook his body.

"The war was over, ya' see," he began. "It had been declared over just that day, but it takes a long time to get the ball rolling, to start movin' us outta there." He coughed and coughed. "We're still lyin' up in them old trenches in France. Well, every night, a different soldier has to take his turn to go out and get us some chickens for our supper and that night it's my turn. We're sittin' not far from a farm, so I sneak over there and just as I'm crawling over a ridge I come face to face with a German boy about my own age. By instinct, we both cock our guns into each other's face. Now I'm thinkin', 'Hey! This war is over. I don't have to kill this boy and he don't have to kill me. But how do I know what he's thinkin'?'"

I looked around the room at the faces of my other aunts and uncles and my grandparents. They looked a little strained, a little sad. Their spirited stories and laughter had been dampened since Uncle Willis had arrived. Some of the other uncles drank, but would never have appeared drunk before their parents and probably not in the presence of their sisters either. They were all very sad about Willis' life and it was clear that they had all heard this story before. But I had not.

Uncle Willis continued. "We stand there like that for a long time, staring at each other. Finally, I make a move with my other arm. I hold up my hand and make a V with two fingers. I'm trying to tell him that I don't speak no German and he don't speak no English, but we probably both want to get out of there alive. He looks relieved and lowers his gun, and I lower mine. He motions to me that he's lookin' for chickens and I laugh and motion that I'm doing the same. We both get our chickens and get on outta there, back to our regiments."

Uncle Willis was not aggressively affectionate in the way of his brothers. He probably sensed, correctly, that I was afraid of him. At home we did not associate with anyone who drank alcohol, even socially, so I was terrified of anyone who smelled of it. His drinking and the fact that he spoke very loudly due to returning form the war hearing-impaired caused me, as well as my brothers and sister, to shrink from Uncle Willis. We knew him less well than our other aunts and uncles. This bothered our mother. She wanted us to love the Willis that *she* knew — the Willis who she said was the smartest person she'd ever known, the Willis who had once pitifully asked if God could forgive a boy who had killed in a war.

He was born in 1924, the first son of his parents and given the name Willis Augustus, Willis being his father's assumed middle name and Augustus being the male rendering of my grandmother's favoured "Aunt Gussie."

He was the only one of the Smith children to grow up without a "partner," each of the others having had a sibling close in age of the same gender. Willis arrived between Edith and Ethel and Sidney and Olie and was considered by some of his family to have been a loner.

I have been told that during the family prayer meetings in which all of the Smiths participated, Willis sat outside on the porch and assured passersby that the noise inside was the result of a game of cowboys that the children were engaged in.

Willis lied about his age to join the Canadian Army and the Second World War effort. He was seventeen years old and the war seemed a great opportunity to him. His efforts at school had been very promising, but he believed, as did other young Black men of his time, that with or without a high school diploma he would spend his life at one of three occupations; pinning chickens, shining shoes or working as a porter on the railroad. Seeing no point to an education for its own sake, he left school for the war, which offered pay along with what he perceived to be dignity and prestige.

There is a letter from him that has survived the years in its yellowed, torn envelope, stamped

July 1/43
L/BdrSmith W.A. L-51508
Canadian Army Overseas

To my mother he had written:

Dear Pauline,
Just a line to say hello and to let you know that the kid brother is still around.

I hear that you are going to high school now. I do hope that you go all the way through with it. With a start like that if you keep it up you will be able to make something of yourself.

As it is you'll probably laugh yourself sick at my writing and spelling.

I don't think I've changed much since I left home. I haven't got (sic) any taller though I have filled out a bit. I'm still as dumb as I used to be.

Mr. Darling [his Regina school principal] *wrote me a letter and gave me the low down on all the kids I went to school with. They are either all married or in one or the other of the armed forces.*

I am trying to write this letter in the kitchen of a Wop [sic] house. With the wops jabbering away and the boys playing crib it's a pretty tough go. I have been playing bridge all night and so as usual don't feel much like writing but I have made a resolution to write two letters per day and I'm going to live up to it if it kills me.

It likely will.

See what I mean when I say the noise makes it hard to concentrate. The Capt. and one of the boys are playing right at my elbow and with fifteen two and fifteen four and a pair is six I can't think at all.

Well, Paul. I'm getting pretty tired and it's getting late so I'll close for now.

Love,

Willis

My mother was late or nearly late for school every day that Willis was away. She would walk slowly to the end of her block on Ottawa Street in Regina and wait until the telegram delivery boy came into view on his bicycle. She would stand and wait until she was certain that he had bypassed her block, then run the rest of the way to school. Occasionally, he would turn onto Ottawa Street, in which case she would watch until he made his way to another, less fortunate family.

One day, unbelieving, she saw the messenger continue to the very end of the block, where the Smith family lived, and hop down from his bicycle in front of that big, rambling house. He leaned the handlebars against the fence and walked along the crooked boards of the sidewalk. He raised his fist to bang on the door, then my mother began to run. It was the standard way in which a family received news of a death then, in a black-edged envelope from a stranger on a bicycle. The telegram, bearing the news of my grandfather's mother's death was still unopened in her mother's hand when she burst through the door.

When a loved one is ill, or far away and in danger, it is odd to receive news of another death, a different death that, another day, would have carried its own sadness. Instead of grief, there is a moment of euphoria upon discovering the reprieve, that the death is not the most dreaded news that one had been awaiting.

There is then, of course, the task of disguising the relief, a task that my grandmother and mother shared that day.

Twenty years later, in my grandparent's living room, I looked at my mother's face as she looked at her brother as he rambled drunkenly. He had other stories to tell. He'd had a best friend, a buddy over there, whose death had left my uncle feeling lost, abandoned. He had written the boy's family, to tell them that their son had not suffered.

He had met a beautiful French girl.

My mother was looking at Willis as though he had died in Europe, as though it was not really him sitting there among us. At home, she always spoke of him in the past tense. He'd had so much promise. He had been so handsome. He used to sing like a bird. She was looking at him as though his life was past.

He coughed and laughed and told another story. His only injury, he said, the only damage he'd sustained through the entire war was a bite on his leg from a dog.

I'm not sure if even he believed that.

Ottawa Street

. . . they raised their family with their full hearts . . .
and the house was filled with a great deal of laughter . . .

*M*y mother and her family so romanticized the years that they spent in Regina that it was impossible to believe that any other life in any other time could compare to those years. The Waltons themselves would have blushed to imply that poverty could be so much fun. The depression, the war, illness, prejudice, all these were just obstacles that they withstood and conquered together.

The rosy haze through which they looked back at their years as a happy group living together under one roof was charming and contagious to we, their children. There are few among my large group of cousins who could not repeat and act out the various dramas from those years, or who grow tired of hearing "the stories" that we first heard in our grandparents' living room.

My grandparents started their large family on a farm near Lashburn, Saskatchewan. When my grandfather's father became ill and was taken to Regina General Hospital in 1925, they took their three small children, Ethel, Edith and Willis to Regina to be near him. Although my grandfather did not realize it then, he would never return to farming.

The family moved frequently at first, always, as the family grew, in search of larger premises. They went from Retallack Street, to Arthur Street, to Edward Street, from there to Coronation

Park, then to Broad Street and at last to Ottawa street. The big, old house on Ottawa Street with its reasonable six dollars per month rent was where they settled for a number of years and where dwell most of their childhood memories.

I have seen a photograph of the house, a yellow, faded picture in which my mother and her twin, Pearl, are standing at the end of a weatherscarred wooden walkway. They are wearing cotton print dresses, ankle socks and black shoes with buckles. It was taken on a windy day; Pearl's hair is flying. The house behind them is like other prairie houses of the thirties that I have seen. It is large and a little askew, in need of a paint job. It has a porch.

The house was at the end of Ottawa Street. Beyond the Smiths was the prairie, no trees, just the hardy grasses and the gophers. When it rained, they were surrounded by mud of the sort that would swallow you, but when it was dry they had a boundless playground and a shortcut to school.

There was a well in back of the house, a luxury which saved them the inconvenience of walking several blocks, as most of their neighbors did, to draw their water.

To their joy, the house proved to be actually large enough for their needs, with three bedrooms up and one down, a cellar with a big, black, coal and wood stove, a living room, dining room and a large kitchen. They kept two large tables in the kitchen, an oval one that could seat the eleven of them and another

Pauline and Pearl at the well, Ottawa Street, 1940.

square table that my grandmother and her second daughter Edith used for baking. In the middle of the room stood the pot-bellied stove. Often, in the evenings, my grandmother would drag the rocking chair in from the living room, hold the twins or the babies,

Bert and Dave, on her lap, the other children would settle themselves around her and she would tell them stories.

Occasionally, when it was very cold, they would stoke the living room stove to try to pump heat throughout the home. There was also a large, rectangular grate in the dining room, around which the Smith children would huddle to get dressed for school in the morning to take advantage of the heat blasting up from the cellar furnace.

It was a very fundamental life that they had. My grandparents struggled to provide basic care, food and clothing, but they raised their family with their full hearts and, from all accounts, the family was a happy one. They loved each other with what seems to be almost ferocity and the house was filled with a great deal of laughter.

My grandfather found a position "pinning" chickens at Canada Packers. In retrospect, although it would appear to have been a job unworthy of his wit or dignity, it is clear that he was not ashamed of it. It was a steady job at a time when many men, especially Black men, found them to be scarce. My grandfather believed that hard work was the foundation around which you built your life and that if you did a job well, you could hold your head up.

The Smith children emulated their parents' attitude toward work. Aside from their chores — drawing water from the well, cutting, chopping and stacking wood, cleaning, cooking and laundry — the entire family congregated in the cellar in the evening, pinning chickens to help meet expenses. In the mid-to-late thirties, pinning a chicken was worth five cents and the Smith children were allowed to pocket two cents from every nickel that they earned.

After dinner, my mother and Pearl would dawdle as long as they could over the dishes, knowing that when they were finished they would join the rest of the family below over the mounds of feathers and the pimply bodies of the poultry. The pinning was a task made bearable only by their mother's singing, or stories, or talk of what they would do with their earned money when the exhibition wagons rolled into town.

On weekends or warm summer days, the entire family moved out into the prairie, carrying magnets with which to scour for metal and sacks to fill with rags and bottles. Often they would stop to pick flowers to decorate the house. Returning home they would pool the lot, and Grandpa would build a bonfire at the back of the house, to burn the casing from the bits of wire that they had found.

In this way, they managed to survive the depression.

Once or twice, though, during the thirties, my grandfather was laid off from the Packers and during those months, no amount of wire or bottles gathered from the fields was enough to feed eleven people. In desperation, he would walk up and down Regina streets, knocking on doors to enquire if there was any chore that he might do.

During one of these lean periods, Regina settled into a very cold turn of weather. The Smiths ran short of wood and there was no coal to be had anywhere. My grandmother, without saying where she was going, left the house one night and made her way to the rail yard, some blocks away, where sat piles of railroad ties, rotting in the wind and the rain, year after year.

She was nervous, not because she was an unwavering Christian on her way out to "steal" a railroad tie. God, she believed, would understand a mother taking an otherwise useless piece of wood to keep her children from freezing. She was more concerned with the men who owned the railyard and their "dog in the manger" attitude. Her old neighbor on Broad Street, she had heard, had been charged with theft for committing just the crime that she was about to commit.

My grandmother reached the barbed wire that separated the railyard from the field and the street beyond it, gathered her skirt and coat in one arm and somehow squeezed through. She waded through the snow to a pile of ties and pushed a couple of them aside until she found one that looked relatively dry. Breathing heavily, both from exertion and apprehension, she dragged it away from the tracks toward the section of fence that she had come through.

Just before she reached the fence a footstep appeared out of the darkness and a beam of light blinded her. My grandmother peered into the light, unable to make out the face of her confronter.

"Drop it this side of the tracks, lady," his voice said, "and I won't report you."

"All right," my grandmother said and let her tie fall into the snow. She crossed the fence and walked a block, rounding a corner and waiting until she was sure that the guard had gone.

She quickly returned to the railyard, snatched the nearest tie, pushed it under the barbed wire and dragged and carried it as best she could back to the house on Ottawa Street.

Having given birth to her previous five children at home, my grandmother was sent to the hospital for the first time in 1930, to bear her twins, my mother Pauline, and Pearl. They were so small that the attending doctor assured Grandma that they wouldn't survive. She begged to be allowed to take them home and the doctor consented, saying that there was nothing that could be done for them in the hospital.

Once home with the baby girls, my grandmother nestled each of them into a blanket in a shoe box and placed them on the open door of the oven for warmth. She called her ten-year-old daughter Ethel and her eight-year-old daughter Edith to see their sisters.

"You pick one, Ethel," she said, "and that will be your baby to help Mama look after. Edith will care for the other one."

Ethel looked at Pauline first. "That one's ugly," she said upon seeing the scrawny, wrinkled creature that was my mother. "I don't want it." She then peeked in at Pearl, who had been born first and was only slightly less shrivelled. Ethel sighed. "I'll take this one I guess."

Thereafter, and indeed to this day, Pearl has "belonged" to her sister Ethel and my mother retains her affinity for her sister Edie.

As can be said of most twins, Pauline and Pearl's lives were so entwined that one cannot think of one without thinking of the other. Alike in some ways, dramatically dissimilar in others, they adapted their personalities to complement one another.

My mother was quiet, but Pearl talked enough for the two of them, and very rapidly. I have been told that when a kindly old lady once asked them what they were called, Pearl rattled off their names so quickly that the old woman replied, "Pearlpline, what a lovely name!" then turned to my mother and asked, "And what is your name, dear?"

Pearl, although quite bright, was not interested in school. She benefited from my mother's serious nature, asking for and receiving permission to borrow homework and school assignments. This arrangement was satisfactory until my mother, who was "studious," was promoted to a higher grade, despite a heart condition, the result of rheumatic fever, that caused her to miss weeks of school at a time.

My mother was less fun-loving, less wild than her twin. She wanted to travel as an evangelist when she reached adulthood, whereas Pearl was less content to live out her life in "the four corners of the church." She strained against the restrictions of their upbringing, unsuccessfully pleading with her parents to be allowed to go to Regina Beach on the occasional Sunday, instead of always "church, church, church," the Regina Apostolic Mission.

Fortunately for my spirited aunt, she and my mother enjoyed the company of a group of their peers at the mission, a collection of young girls that they still quaintly refer to as their "gang."

The Smith twins, Marjorie McDermott, Sylvie Osler (who was also their neighbor on Ottawa Street), Sophie Rausch, Elva Johnson, Lorraine Wallace, Irene Turner and Mamie Sweet comprised a loose sort of club that lasted well into their late teens. The nine of them once persuaded their pastor, "Brother" Story, to let them play instruments in the church orchestra, although only Pearl and Sylvia demonstrated even the remotest glimmer of musical aptitude. They were each given a guitar and instructions to follow the chords of the church musicians. Their efforts resulted in more embarrassed laughter than music. Pearl avoided meeting my mother's eye, knowing that if she did they would be unable to maintain any semblance of composure. Finally, when she could stand it no longer, she raised her head to look at her twin, only to see that instead of laughing, my mother was in obvious pain.

She nudged Elva, who was sitting between them and said, "Ask Paul what's wrong."

Elva whispered to my mother and my mother looked at Pearl, pointing to her heart. At the end of the service, the group of friends gathered around my mother, uncertain of what to do. Earlier, they had made plans to walk home from church and had used their bus fare to buy candy. It was clear now that my mother could not walk the two odd miles to Ottawa Street and between the nine of them they had only five cents, enough for one bus fare.

"I don't think you should go alone," Pearl said.

"I think we should tell Brother Story," Sophie Rausch said.

My mother, never wishing to draw attention to her illness, waved them off. "I'm feeling better already," she lied. "I'll be fine once I'm on the bus."

They walked her slowly to the bus stop and waited with her there until the Red and Green Line bus arrived, then watched anxiously from the street as she made her way to a seat.

The bus driver, who frequently transported members of the Smith family, turned to stare at my mother who had seated herself two rows behind and to the right of him. "Are you all right?" he asked her.

She nodded and looked out the window.

She grew more and more ill as they bumped along, and was aware of the driver watching her through his rear view mirror. Still, when he halted the bus at the schoolyard just beyond Ottawa Street, she stubbornly refused his offer of assistance, or to let another passenger walk her to her house. She walked erect around a corner of the school building, where she knew she was out of sight of the bus. A moment or two later, she heard it pull away.

"A minute to rest," she thought to herself, "and then I'll use the fence to help me past the school, and then I'll just have the field to cross."

The distance from the school to her house, which she normally would have covered running in five minutes on a warm, dry evening such as it was, seemed far to her. Gathering what energy she could muster, she leaned against the school fence and slowly began to edge along the perimeter of the grounds.

She remembered a dream that her mother had described to the family just days before, in which she, Pauline, had been calling to her parents. The dream had awakened her, my grandmother had said, it seemed that real.

"I wish they could hear me now if I called," my mother thought.

She released the fence and took her first step onto the open prairie which lay between her and her home. She took another step, then stopped. She pushed her foot ahead one more time and felt a knife in her chest.

"I'll crawl," she said aloud.

My mother cautiously lowered herself to the earth and began to move on her hands and knees. She realized at that point that she should have swallowed her embarrassment and accepted the bus driver's help, that she had never been as ill before.

"Too late, too late, too late," her thoughts chanted as she lifted her arms and legs again and again.

In the house, my grandmother, passing the living room on her way to bed, saw my grandfather standing at the window. "Is there something wrong, George?" she asked him.

"No," he said, turning his head toward her. "No, I don't think so," but he was frowning. "You go on to bed. I'll just sit here until the girls come."

He waited in the rocking chair in the dark until he heard a thump, then hurried to the door.

My mother had pulled herself to the bottom of the stairs. "Daddy," she said weakly.

Due to her illness, my mother missed out on the school's field day that year, leaving the way open for Pearl to bring home all the ribbons. (They usually split them.) She also missed several weeks' worth of church services, but no matter, Pearl would return from each meeting and re-enact them from start to finish. My mother would then know who had prayed, who had sung badly, who spat when they testified and the highlights of the sermon, without her sister ever having mentioned a name, such was Pearl's talent for mimicry. So hard would my mother laugh that my grandparents would intervene, concerned firstly that imitating God's people was disrespectful and secondly that my mother's heart would "take another spell."

As for staying abreast of events at school, my mother depended upon her brother Olie. As part of the school's policy of combining two grades in one classroom, Olie, who was two years older, found himself sharing a teacher with my mother that year. He brought her work home and informed her of each day's events.

Olie was the bad boy of his family, a title which he will still ruefully admit to. Perhaps a result of having been born exactly in the middle of a very large family, he always made certain that no one could ever, ever ignore the presence of Olie Smith.

When my mother, Pearl, Olie, and Sidney, who was just a bit older than Olie, planned any activity that required partners, my mother paired with Olie, and Pearl with Sidney.

Whether or not my mother was thrown together with her roguish older brother willingly, they grew to have a special affinity for one another that has lasted. They were an example of the ability of opposites to attract; he often in trouble of one sort or another; she obedient and compliant to an unusual degree.

There is no end to the number of stories that my mother will relate about Olie and the vexations he caused as a youth. If she is to be believed, he was a hellion, able to work his classmates into a frenzy of disobedience and outright mutiny and send the teacher, weeping, from the room.

He would fight at school, she said, and shout into the teacher's ear when the unfortunate creature went around to test their voices for choir.

One day Miss Jetminson asked my mother to remain after class to help clean the boards. However, when her classmates had filed out and my mother marched to the front of the classroom to begin the chore, the teacher interrupted her.

"Pauline, I really didn't want you to help with the chalkboards tonight. I'm having a little problem and I was wondering if you might be willing to help me?"

She posed it as a question, so my mother, who was standing with her head down, nodded slightly.

Miss Jetminson continued. "Do you think you might take a note home to your mother for me?"

My mother, aware that the note would concern her brother Olie, took a moment to think it through. She was fond of her brother, but he was being awfully hard on the delicate, pretty teacher who was almost defenseless against him. Perhaps if their mother spoke to Olie, without telling Daddy, Olie would get away without a strapping and would be persuaded to settle down.

She agreed to take the note and Miss Jetminson pressed the damp envelope that she had been clutching into my mother's hand.

"We won't tell anyone, okay Pauline?" she begged. "Just our little secret."

My mother stuffed the envelope into the pocket of the dress that she was wearing and left the classroom. She ventured into the hallway, with some trepidation. Earlier, Olie had been the last to file out of the room and had cast a long glance her way.

Everything looked clear and she made her way down the long hall. She reached the end, and preparing to run the entire distance to Ottawa Street, she burst through the doorway, only to be stopped short by the menacing presence of her brother who was waiting there.

"Where you goin', Sis?" he drawled out of the corner of his mouth.

He, unlike her, was very calm.

"I'm not going anywhere," the innocent Pauline said, breathing heavily.

"Aren't you headin' home?"

My mother, head down, nodded.

"What you got in your pocket, Sis?"

(This question always reminded me of Gollum's question to Bilbo, as they sat in the bowels of Middle Earth, Bilbo turning the ring over and over in his fingers the way my mother fingered the note, Gollum repeating over and over, "What has it got in its pocketses?" The difference was that Olie knew the answer to the riddle.)

"Better give me that note, Paul."

Olie acquired the note somehow, not through actual force, but by exercising the power that older brothers have over younger sisters.

My mother repeated this story in Winnipeg for the entertainment of her family, gleefully acting out the parts of herself, her brother and the pathetic Miss Jetminson. The only person who enjoyed it more than she was Olie, who laughed his staccato, bleating laugh until tears rolled from beneath his glasses.

That day, he tacked a postscript onto the story.

"I bumped into Miss Jetminson here in Winnipeg a few years after I'd left Regina," he said. "I walked up to her, smiling and called her by name. She looked at me and turned her head." He tapped out his cigarette. "I said, 'Don't you remember me, Miss Jetminson, I'm Olie Smith.' She looked at me again, still not smiling. 'I remember you,' she said. 'I remember you very well.'" He bleated again.

Although I imagine that Uncle Olie grinned, shrugged and sauntered away after her rebuff, I'm certain that he was surprised and even hurt. If he prided himself on his reputation as a firebrand, he doubly prided himself on his charm.

Everyone liked him, everyone found his antics amusing, with the obvious exception of little Miss Jetminson from the Regina school.

In Sharon's Room

*When someone calls you "nigger" they are
really talking about themselves . . .*

After leaving Winnipeg that spring, my parents decided that
we would drive until my father could drive no longer, then stop
overnight at a motel, a decision which carried us to Indian Head,
Saskatchewan. We children, still excited about our holiday, huddled between the thin sheets and lumpy mattresses that our way-
stop offered and giggled long past our usual bedtime.

Finally, following the command from our mother to "settle it,"
we slept. The next morning, the motel's gas pump attendant told
my father that a storm warning had been issued to travellers on the
number one, recommending that motorists east of Calgary take
shelter where they could and wait for the tempest to pass.

The sky over Indian Head was clear and my parents, who knew
that weather reports on the prairies change from hour to hour,
decided we would travel on.

By the time we reached Medicine Hat, the worst storm I have
ever seen, before or since, had completely enveloped us. We were
dimly aware that along the side of the road, stranded and even
overturned vehicles lay, their panicked occupants waiting to be
rescued. Our old car, which had been moving at the minimum
possible speed for more than an hour, finally trembled and gave

up the attempt, leaving us to join the numbers parked along the highway's shoulder at crazy angles.

In the ensuing hours, we found ourselves abandoning our vehicle and being separated from one another. A stranger would appear at the window, saying that he had room for one or two, and one or two of us would go, with hastily formed plans to meet again at the next town. My heart sank as I watched my mother climb into a car and be driven away, clutching my brother Darcy who was little more than three-months-old. Too late, we realized that she had left her purse and the baby's bag of diapers and bottles with us.

Somehow, with the luck that will occasionally save people from a terrible circumstance made worse by foolish decisions, we all were reunited safely, not in the next town as planned, but in the next one along the route. It came out, as we each related our piece of the adventure, that in the madness my five-year-old sister Noël had been sent alone with a carful of strangers and had been left at a gas station for hours, unattended.

My mother, twenty-five years later, still recalls this event with a shrill, nervous laugh and usually punctuates discussion of it by saying, "Well, the Lord looks after the dumb and the stupid."

For myself, I remember that later that night when I could see Calgary's lights, I couldn't wait to get home, so that I could tell the story to Sharon.

*D*espite being eight years my senior, Sharon not only tolerated my constant presence with complete patience, but she somehow managed to convince me that she drew as much pleasure from our association as did I.

She was my cousin, daughter to Aunt Edie and Uncle Andrew, and older sister to Phillip, Danny, Beverly and Brian.

They lived in a house that must have seemed small to the seven of them, especially considering the needy people that they often took in, but to me it was large enough to harbor many secrets, it was familiar and warmly faded. The house looked like a tired, very old woman trying to maintain her posture, but wanting to relax, to sag a little. It was in an older part of the city, only steps away from Seventeenth Avenue, the most urbane of streets.

The charm of the house was its age. It had a cellar, which one could enter through a trap door in the kitchen floor. The cellar was very dark and I ventured there only once or twice, creeping down the steep staircase to gaze at the rows of jars containing pickled and syrupy things.

Another steep set of stairs led to the bedrooms and bathroom upstairs and to my favourite place, a windowed balcony where I could settle myself with a book and have the sun pour over me.

Upon occasion, if I thought no one would know, I went into my aunt and uncle's room. It was always the same. There was the bedspread with the tassels that hung, the throw rugs on the hardwood floor, the female ambience to the room — the only clue that my uncle resided there

Sharon, age 16

being the presence of his well-thumbed Bible on the dresser beside the tins of talcum powder.

The room that Sharon shared with Beverly, and another that was occupied by their brothers, was atop yet another crazily steep flight of stairs, a space that must have been, at one time, the attic.

These rooms, far from the rest of the house, were ideal for private conversation. If you were to attempt to climb the narrow stairwell, you would be heard as soon as your foot touched the first step. Even should you try to listen from the bottom of the stairs, the creaky floorboards would betray your presence.

I passed numerous hours in these rooms, sometimes with my two older brothers and Brian in the boys' room, but their conversation consisted largely of one tale of their bravado atop another.

My sister and I preferred to visit Sharon and Bev's room, where they would comb our hair and we would glimpse their exotic world that included perfume, white lipstick, girdles and the intoxicating music of Sam and Dave, the Temptations, Joe Tex, Ben E. King, and Solomon Burke. There were few greater rewards in my young life than being invited to spend the night in that room.

One such evening, Sharon and I sat crosslegged on her bed, which was nestled into a nook created by the slanted ceiling of the attic and the wall. I was comfortable sitting there, but Sharon, who at that time had attained nearly all of her eventual five-feet-three inches of height, was hunched over.

We were cracking and eating sunflower seeds.

"Rid swore today," I told her. (Rid, or Riddy, was what we called my brother Richard.)

Although by no means an insophisticate, Sharon was still a minister's daughter and was intrigued by this. She cocked an eyebrow.

"Really? What did he say?"

"I'm not going to say it!"

"Well, spell it then," she urged me.

"It starts with 'h'," I said.

"Is the next letter 'e'?" she asked, leaning forward.

I nodded.

"Is the next letter 'l'?" Her voice had become almost a squeal and her eyes were bright.

"No." I shook my head.

She leaned back and frowned, disappointed.

"What is it then?"

"K," I said.

"K? Heck isn't a swear word," She laughed.

I looked down, pretending to search the foil bag for seeds that had already lost their shell. I was a trifle embarrassed at my gaffe, but relieved nonetheless to learn that my brother had not actually cursed.

After a time, I spoke again. "Sharon?"

"Uhhm mmm?"

"What does nigger mean?"

"It doesn't mean anything."

I did not reply and I did not look up, so she continued.

"It means that the person saying it is ignorant."

"I know." I had heard that a hundred times. "But what does it really mean in the dictionary?"

"It's not in the dictionary, honey." Her tone was very gentle. "Who's been calling you nigger?"

"The Webber boys," I said, whispering.

I began to cry and she pulled me to her.

The Webber boys were part of the largest, cruelest family that I knew. Recently, they had taken to intercepting me when I was playing with my dolls.

They would tear off the dolls' clothing and fling them into the street, and then hurl the dreaded words, "Nigger! Blackie!"

"Do you know what it means?" Sharon was rocking me and humming. "It means that the person saying it is a nigger. When someone calls you nigger they are really talking about themselves."

The swaying motion was soothing, her humming was very self-assured. I was comforted by this new knowledge, that the Webber boys were making fools of themselves, but were too dim to realize it.

"I'm tired," I said to my older cousin.

"You go to sleep," she said. She pulled the quilt and placed the pillow that she had been leaning on underneath my head. She quietly left the room after switching the table lamp on, familiar as she was with my dislike of dark places. She extinguished the overhead light and did not close the door.

I was very safe.

The Great-aunts

*I was daunted by the aggressive confidence
with which this pack of aunts stalked around . . .*

The following day, Sharon braided my hair and helped me to
dress in a new skirt and sweater that my mother had sent along for
me to wear. The great-aunts were coming from Edmonton for a
visit.

I encountered Daisy and my grandfather's other three living
sisters infrequently, perhaps once or twice in a three year period
and when I did see them it was almost always for an occasion
which demanded that they all be there, together like an inseparable
and invincible gang.

The four great-aunts seemed to me to be important people,
having semi-mythic proportions. They wore expensive coats,
lipstick and perfume, but it was their elaborate hats which in-
timidated me most. They were very handsome women, all of them
fair-skinned like my grandfather and their hooked noses always
reminded me that the family was said to have had Cree connections
in Oklahoma.

I was daunted by the aggressive confidence with which this
pack of aunts stalked around. I behaved in their presence with the
semi-mute obedience and respect they would expect from one of
"Son's" grandchildren. ("Son" was what they called my

grandfather, because, I once overheard Daisy saying, "That's what Momma and Papa called him.")

The great-aunts, 1943. Left to right: Bessie, Drucilla, Mary, Maude and Bertha. Daisy is missing from the picture.

That day, as was their usual practice, they encircled and dissected me as though I couldn't hear them and then interrogated me.

"Don't she look just like Reen'?" one of them said and the others nodded or replied, "Hhhn uhn uhn, don't she though." They admired my grandmother and were pleased enough that I resembled her rather than their brother George.

"Got the Smith eyes, though," another of them said.

"Do you do good work at school?" Drucilla or Maude asked.

I nodded.

"Do you know who we are?" another one asked.

"Aunt Daisy and Aunt Maude and Aunt Drucilla and Aunt Sis," I replied shyly. "Aunt Mary and Aunt Bessie aren't here because they're in Heaven."

They were satisfied and all nodded together.

"You're a good girl, aren't you?" Daisy was the spokesperson for the group and it was usually she who addressed me.

I said yes. Just then Sharon interceded on my behalf, poking her head into the archway of the dining room. "I'm going to the store with Beverly, baby. Do you want to come?"

Much relieved, I hurried to my feet. The great-aunts caught me. All of them smiling, they kissed me and then dismissed me.

Freed, I gladly took my leave of them, not knowing, or caring, that one day the great-aunts, especially Daisy, would be important to me.

The March

. . . although I had only a vague understanding of what Martin Luther King had actually done . . . I felt changed by his death . . .

I knew that my mother had been deeply shaken by the assassination of John Kennedy, in part because she believed him to be a friend to Black people. I was dimly aware that while I was spending my summers dodging trains on the Twin Bridges and gathering herbs from the hills to make "perfume," Black people in America were rioting. I had heard of Martin Luther King Jr. Every time he appeared on the evening news, my mother remarked upon how much he resembled her brother Willis and related a story from the late forties. Her co-worker and friend from the Army and Navy in Regina had taken a vacation in the southern states. Upon his return he proudly informed her that he had ridden at the back of the buses, to demonstrate sympathy for, and solidarity with Black people. (He was White.) My mother laughed and asked him if he had also spent time in jail. With the simplistic view that children have, I believed that King's purpose would be accomplished if he could somehow secure the right of American Blacks to ride at the front of public transportation.

Although the struggles of Black Americans had very little impact on my day-to-day life, after 1966 I became less comfortable in my White world. Naivete is rarely permanent and mine began to slip away when cracks started appearing in that world, cracks that eventually became gulfs between me and the things I had formerly cherished.

One day my two best friends began to ridicule the Black music and musicians I had tried to introduce to our self-taught dance classes.

"I hate that crap," one of them said, and the other agreed.

Hurt, I gathered my records and left them. I walked home along the railroad tracks, feeling lonely and inexplicably frightened. Why had they been so vitriolic? Their attack on the music that I was growing to love seemed to carry a message other than a simple dislike of a few songs.

I recalled a recent incident that I had pushed out of my mind. One of my friends had forgotten that she had left me waiting on the telephone, allowing me to inadvertently eavesdrop on a conversation that she had with her mother. She informed her mother that our mutual friend, Ricky Hayes, had given her his friendship ring to wear. Her mother had said that it was all right to be friends with Black people, but that one didn't date "them." I recalled being surprised and confused by my friend's mother's admonishment. In the six or seven years that I had been friends with her daughter, I would not have guessed that this woman's body harboured one bigoted bone.

As I crept toward adolescence, barriers that seemed to have something to do with race were going up in relationships that I had counted on.

Shortly after the murder of Martin Luther King in 1968, some local people, Black and White, organized a march to honour him.

During the lunch break at school that day, a classmate named Laura informed me that she was planning to attend the march and asked if she would see me there.

I said yes, keeping hidden the fact that I had been unaware of plans for the march.

Later that afternoon, I received permission from my mother to participate. She then asked if I was aware of the controversy surrounding the planned march, and informed me that my Uncle Andrew had denied the organizers permission to use his church for a memorial service to end the march. The uproar was compounding even as we spoke. A radio personality, aghast that Calgary's only Black minister appeared to be opposed to paying homage to the life of King, had invited him to make his views heard on the radio that afternoon.

I listened to the broadcast, anguished. Citizens called in on the phone-in program, accusing my uncle of various sins, including being an "Uncle Tom." Uncle Andrew seemed unable to make his position clear, and my mother was inexplicably stricken with a fit of nervous laughter.

I knew that as an evangelical minister, Andrew Risby believed that the church was the sacred House of God and was not to be used for political rallies. I also knew that there had been a rumor that some of the older Black teenage boys, disturbed by King's assassination, might "make trouble." Uncle Andrew envisioned rocks being hurled through the church windows and militants screaming rhetoric from its pulpit.

I wanted him to relent, but failing that, I wanted him to try to make himself understood. He did neither, ending the interview by saying that he would have to meet with the church's board of directors before announcing a decision.

When Laura and I and two hundred-odd marchers convened later that evening, after singing a ragged rendition of "We Shall Overcome" (the words of which hardly anyone knew), we set out for the church, with no idea of the reception awaiting us.

Attending the march was my first political act. I was eleven-years-old and although I had only a vague understanding of what Martin Luther King had actually done in his lifetime, I felt changed by his death. That cool spring evening, for the first time, I no longer felt far removed from the toil of other Black people. As I walked along, my mind was divided between thoughts of what King's family would do without him and thoughts of the roasting that Uncle Andrew would take in the press if he refused to receive us at the church.

When we arrived at the Standard Church of America, the church doors were closed. One of the march leaders turned to address the crowd, suggesting that we disperse peacefully and go to our separate homes. I did not fully hear what he was saying, because I was looking at a window high up on the church building that was open three inches, to the inside, on a chain. I could see a brown face peering down at the throng on the street below.

The window slammed and I counted the steps that I knew my cousin Brian would take in his leap from the chair that he had stood on, through the nursery, down the three steps to the door and, in time with my counting, he flung it wide. Behind him, with a welcoming smile, stood Uncle Andrew.

A reporter clicked and flashed. The next day, Brian appeared in the newspaper, his eyes and the church doors wide open.

Little Big Man

*She often said that I was the lucky one because we laughed
a lot at my house, but to me she was the fortunate one . . .*

*I*n the months and years following the march, Laura became
my most trusted friend. We understood the same music. We felt
the same pain. She, unlike others of our peerage, was precociously
concerned with important issues.

One winter evening in 1970, I walked down 70th street to what
we referred to as "the cut in the road," turned left and continued
to the railroad tracks, on my way to visit her. It was deep winter.
Although I had left home immediately after clearing away the
supper dishes, it was already dark. Still, it was mild for a winter
evening and I was in no hurry.

The walk through the field was always a pleasure. There was
something satisfying about being alone, the quiet, about lifting the
barbed wire and squeezing through and bounding over the rails.
Sometimes I would stop briefly to examine the stones around the
tracks for bits of fool's gold but that particular evening, because
of the dark, I did not.

I half-slid down the hill beyond the tracks and through the thick
woods that lined Laura's back yard. I knocked on the door.

Laura opened it, greeted me and led me directly to her room.

Laura's house was always quiet and lonely feeling. She had an
older sister who was too consumed by make-up and her boyfriend

to be of much interest to Laura. She also had an older brother, whom I had never met, that she worshiped, but he lived in another city. Her parents were very polite to me, but it was obvious that they were perplexed by their youngest child. I believe they thought her very serious and unusual.

We closed the bedroom door behind us. The room was lit by candles and two red pinpricks of flame from some incense that she was burning. She was playing James Taylor's "Sweet Baby James" on her stereo.

She had made some tea in a clay pot which she flavoured with honey and lemon. She offered me a cup, I took it, settled into a chair and put my feet up on her bed.

"It's not bad out," I said, "but this tea sure feels good on my cold hands."

"Wind chill," she replied.

We listened silently to "Fire and Rain."

When it was finished, Laura said, "I've been thinking about changing my name."

"Oh? To what?"

"Nothing really different. I thought I might change the spelling to Lara and just, you know, change the pronunciation."

"Lara," I repeated it. "I like that. Are you going to make it official?"

"No. My parents would go nuts. I'll just introduce myself as Lara from now on."

I nodded.

"A few really close friends could call me Lara. You could."

"Sure."

Laura went to the stereo and replaced James Taylor with Marvin Gaye's "What's Goin' On."

She often said that I was lucky because we laughed a lot at my house, but to me she was the fortunate one. She had the stereo, a room to herself, posters on the walls, the huge backyard with the forest and the fire pit.

I poured myself another cup of tea. "Do you know what I find myself thinking about a lot these days?" Laura asked me.

"What?"

"Sex."

Again, I nodded.

"Do you ever think about it?" She looked embarrassed.

"Sometimes."

"You'll probably think this is strange, but I've been thinking about Gordon. Weird, eh?"

"No. Just because he's skinny doesn't mean he isn't sexy."

Laura relaxed and took a long sip from her teacup.

I wondered to myself what Gordon would think if he knew that brown-eyed, brown-haired, prematurely voluptuous Laura had been fantasizing about him.

Laura spoke again.

"My brother took me to see 'Little Big Man' last week."

"Your brother sounds great."

"Yes, he is. I've told him about you. He said to tell you 'Right on'." She was silent for so long that I thought she was through speaking of her brother, but when she resumed talking she said, "He really believes in peace, you know?"

I grunted, indicating that I understood. "How was the movie?"

"It was good. You wouldn't believe the things the white man did to the Indians."

"Sure I would."

"Anyway, at the end, I stood up and renounced my Whiteness."

I laughed. "What do you mean?"

"I stood up and looked at all the White people around me, and they seemed really disgusting. I said, 'White man, I am no longer one of you' and walked out."

I couldn't conceal my amusement. I laughed again.

Laura looked hurt. "I wish you wouldn't make fun of me."

"I'm not. I'm not making fun at all. I'm laughing because I believe you. I really believe that you did that."

She smiled. "I guess it is funny. Glenn laughed too."

"I'd best go," I said. "I've got to be home by 9:30, Lara."

"I'll walk you to the tracks." She bent to cover the incense pots and the sweet threads of smoke drifted through her hair and into her serious eyes.

Living in the Middle

*Too many years in a White world had caused me to forget,
once too often, that I was Black...*

*V*arious minorities will occasionally experience periods of
trendiness in North America. An event or string of events in a
foreign country will trigger the onset of a phenomenon such as the
Nehru jacket. Fashions in hair and clothing will reflect the influence of the season's foreign culture of choice. Suddenly, even
people who despise cooked fish will know everything there is to
know about sushi. Japanese models will sprinkle the pages of
Vogue.

In the early seventies, North American Blacks experienced our
episode of modishness, or what we referred to then as being "in."

Even our neighbors in Bowness had heard that "Black is
Beautiful." Comics like George Carlin and groups like the Rolling
Stones were bragging about their Black connections. White bands
wore afros, White students at Bowness High School followed suit
and played blues on their harmonicas in the courtyard.

It was a shortlived time, but fortunately for me occurred during
my adolescence. While undergoing the standard severe pain of
being fourteen, I had my newly "cool" blackness to give me a sense
of purpose.

I felt noble the night that I decided I would no longer straighten
my hair. I was going natural. Bolstering my confidence was the

shriek of delight that I elicited from Sharon when I informed her of my decision and displayed my afro to her. Her approval more than compensated for the titters that greeted me when I walked into my classroom at school the next day. My resolve to demonstrate that I was "Black and Proud" in the way that James Brown described in his song was only cemented when a classmate shouted "Cheryl, did you stick your finger in an electrical outlet?" and my fellow students burst into laughter.

My older brothers and I had begun what could not actually have been considered dating, as that word implies actually going out somewhere, but what might be considered "pre" dating. Our forays into relationships with the opposing gender consisted of eating lunch with that person in the cafeteria, going to Bowness Park or Market Mall to hold hands during spares, or perhaps meeting on weekends to play records.

The average citizen of Calgary found biracial dating to be a great curiosity and passersby in vehicles would often strain their necks to ogle us if we ventured onto public streets in physical contact with a White friend of the opposite sex.

This was such a frequent occurrence that, in all honesty, I had ceased to take note of it until the advent into my life of a fellow student of Bowness two years older than I, named Brian. I had met Brian at a camp for elementary school students which the two of us had been selected to attend as counsellors. We had been mutually intrigued. He informed me, for some reason, in the early stages of our attraction, that his father and grandfather were bigots. I was taken aback by this pronouncement, but as Brian indicated total disagreement with their views and clearly seemed intent upon pursuing our relationship, I shrugged it off.

When our week in the foothills camp ended and we returned to the city, I noticed that Brian was very disturbed by the stares we encountered on the street, blushing and becoming fidgety. I decided after a week or two that we should discuss his discomfort.

"Doesn't it bother you?" he asked me.

"Well, I don't like it, but what am I supposed to do, run after a car shouting, 'Hey, don't look at us?'"

"I don't know," he replied. "It just gives me the creeps."

We did not return to the topic again.

A week later, Brian did not appear at our usual morning meeting place at the school. When I saw him later, between classes and walked toward him smiling, he ignored me and hurried past. I stood in the hallway, stunned.

Over the next days I retained hope that Brian would explain his actions, but gradually I had to accept that he had rejected me utterly and did not wish to tell me why.

Had his parents learned of our friendship and forbidden it? Had a friend of his chided him regarding me? Was he simply unable to continue tolerating the curiosity of strangers? I do not know the answers to these questions now, nor does Brian know of the tremendous impact that our brief encounter has had upon my life.

Had I been older, or younger, I may have been more rational about my ordeal with Brian. As it was, already crippled by the daily horror of adolescence, I felt as though Brian had pierced my life with a poison dart.

I believed that I had only myself to blame for what had happened. I had trusted when I should not have done so. I had been drifting through my life with closed eyes.

I was not Black enough, I concluded. Too many years in a White world had caused me to forget, once too often, that I was Black and that my blackness was the first thing seen and reacted to by every white person that I met and that many, many people would never see beyond my skin. Whether I liked it or not, the world was Black and White and I had been attempting to live in the middle.

I began to retreat from what I perceived to be "White culture." I immersed myself in the literature of Black authors, became fascinated by the history of Black Americans and was attracted to Black music that reflected a "revolutionary" message. I no longer believed that Canada was a refuge from racism and resented being raised in isolation from other Blacks.

My social circle was drastically pared down. A number of former friends were repelled by my incessant Black consciousness and my refusal to behave any longer as though I were "just one of them." A few friends were supportive of my metamorphosis. I retained the tenacious loyalty of Laura, Aarla Heyden and Clem Martini, who (along with Laura) had refrained from laughing at my afro in the eighth grade.

The gaps in my life created by rapidly vanished acquaintances were filled by the reliable companionship of my sister Noël and my older brother Richard, to whom I had always been very attached. Weekends and school holidays I spent with Sharon, who by now had two small children, the result of an unsuccessful marriage.

Sharon frequently went out in the evening, leaving her little boy and girl in my care. I would wait up for her, no matter how late. I would hear her key turn in the lock and look up from my reading and smile. Her face would light up, she would say, "Hi baby" or "Hi kiddo, how were my children?" I would describe the evening's activities and Sharon would laugh, saying, "You're a better mother than I am."

She did not like to sleep. Looking back, I believe that she must have suffered from insomnia, as she would avoid the notion of night being a time for recumbence by ordering an elaborate meal of steak, baked potato and tossed salad with red cabbage for the two of us from the Four Brothers Restaurant, which was not far from her apartment. She would talk, I would listen, until she saw the sun rising, then looking relieved that the night was past, she would say that we should try to rest.

I believed that I would go mad waiting for the summer to arrive that year. I wanted to be free of school, not to see Brian in the hallways every day, not to hear the yammering of students discussing beer and who had thrown up upon whose mother's flower bed, I wished not to be bored any further by my teachers.

On the last day of school, I rode home on my bicycle alongside my friend Clem, who despite living in another area of Bowness, usually accompanied me as far as my house and stopped long enough for a cold ginger ale.

I was truly happy for the first time in months, the sun was hot on the back of my neck, but there was just enough of a breeze to bring the smell of growing grass to my nostrils.

"Ah, Clem," I said, "It's finally over. I feel like I'm nine years old. I want to sing, 'No more teachers, no more books!'"

"Go ahead. Sing," he said. "What are you going to do for the summer?"

"Hang around for three weeks, sleep in, read, then we're taking the annual car trip to Winnipeg."

"Everybody going?"

"No. Ronny didn't go last year, I don't think he's coming this year. This might be my last year too. It's getting crowded in the car now that we're old."

"I know what you mean. My two older brothers haven't done the summer camping trip with us for two years. Ben and I still like to go. We hike all day while Mom hangs out at the campsite making great food. She doesn't bug us or anything. It's okay."

We had reached my house and had dropped our tenspeeds in the grass in front of the fence. When I emerged from the front door with two icy glasses, Clem had already stretched out on the wooden steps.

"So, when will you leave for the camping trip?" I asked him.

"Couple of days. I still haven't told my parents about getting kicked out of social though. Ma will be in a bad mood for the first while."

"Don't tell her."

"Well, they'll see the incomplete on my report card. Best to tell her myself." I grunted.

We had been studying mores and sanctions in Social Studies two weeks earlier. The unsuspecting teacher had addressed the class in general, asking, "People, does anyone know how to define a more?"

Clem offered an answer. "When the moon's in the sky like a big pizza pie, that's . . . a more."

His perceived insolence and the ensuing laughter from the rest of the class caused the woman to turn purple, her eyes to bulge and her lips to sputter, "Get out!"

She had not seen fit to invite him back for the duration of the school year.

I shook my head. "I can't believe that she wouldn't let you write the final exam so that you could get your mark."

Clem shrugged. "I'll pick it up next year."

We talked a while longer, then Clem slung the heavy pack filled with paraphernalia of a school year over his shoulder and took his leave.

As I had told Clem that I would do, I accomplished little that was noteworthy over the next few weeks. My brother Richard and I played cards late into every night, after shunning Merv Griffin for the more sophisticated David Frost, who featured at least one Black guest on every program. Following gin rummy or cribbage, we ordered Chinese food or baked pizza, then sat in the dark living room whispering and laughing until we heard the thump of the (now-defunct) *Albertan* on the porch. We retrieved the newspaper, perused it, and only then retired to bed.

Each day was the same. Our mother, having been raised with a strong work ethic, feared that her children were displaying early signs of degeneracy, but she said little beyond, "Tch, tch, tch," when we climbed out of bed at 2:00 every afternoon.

The Welcome

In the very beginning, Winnipeg appeared to be welcoming . . .

The family departed for Winnipeg early on the morning of July 23rd, all of us feeling particularly jovial. We had predetermined that we would drive as far as Regina, now that Richard had his learner's licence and would be able to take a shift or two, and that we would stop there for a full day. My mother decided, for reasons unknown to us, that we should all see the house on Ottawa Street where she had grown up, and she had promised that we would then spend the night at a "decent" motel. The two youngest, Darcy and Dion, clamoured that the motel should have a swimming pool, as I had promised to teach them to swim that summer.

I nodded my somewhat timorous agreement, as I contemplated my own limited aquatic talents.

Later that evening, following the sojourn to Ottawa Street, we checked into the motel that was luxurious when compared to the establishments we had rested at in years past (our mother had taken a position as a library clerk in R.B. Bennett Elementary School the year that I turned twelve and we were no longer destitute as we had once been). After the promised swimming lesson with the two younger boys, Richard and I left the family at the motel to explore the surrounding area. We discussed the house on Ottawa Street that we had heard of so many times.

"What did you think of it?" I asked him.

"It's old," he said.

This was true. The house had been old when our mother and aunts and uncles had dwelled there, it was now about as old as anything that I had ever seen.

"I wonder why Mom didn't say anything," Richard mused.

We had, after a time of looking at maps, located the house. Our mother said, "There it is," and we slowed down, then stopped. After a few moments of peering through the car windows, we drove off in silence.

My brother and I walked along, in no hurry, until we encountered a small shopping centre. We entered a variety store, where Richard drifted to the rack of sport magazines and I to a shelf of books. I browsed for a time until something caused me to pause. I took the book from its place and went to my brother.

"Look at this." I nudged him. In my hand was a small book, titled "Black Beauty" that had seemed so incongruously placed among the other books in this Regina corner store, that I had at first been certain that it was an abridged version of the children's novel. Upon investigation, I discovered that the Black model looking out from the cover was indeed portentous of what was inside — page after page of hair, make-up and general beauty advice for Black women. I was stunned. In Calgary, we were still importing hair products from our relatives south of the border, yet there, in Regina I had discovered something that I had not known to exist. I knew that my mother's family had *been* Regina's Black community when they had lived there and I would not have believed that Regina's Black population had swelled by much since that time. Suddenly, Regina seemed far more cosmopolitan than I had thought and I could not wait to return to the motel to share my find with my mother and sister.

Noël had in fact already gone to bed by the time that Richard and I arrived. Mother was sitting alone at the table in the small kitchen, drinking a cup of coffee.

Whispering so as not to wake the others, I told her about my find and showed her the book. She turned its pages, nodding as though it all made perfect sense to her, clearly pleased at the new tone of respect in my attitude toward Regina, the city to which she had always remained loyally affectionate.

Now that we had actually seen Ottawa Street and found the book "Black Beauty," Richard and I prodded our mother for details of what her life there had been like and she complied. The three of us huddled around the wobbly table for some time, talking quietly.

*M*y grandfather worked at the Canada Packers plant in Regina for something like twenty years, perhaps a little more or

Grandfather and Arrenna Smith prior to marriage, 1935.

less. He was industrious, a labourer who would have lived the cliche, "Never missed a day of work for twenty years," were it not for the lay-offs during the depression. I believe that he was proud of his work there, perhaps not of the work itself, but of the act of working, knowing that he sustained his family, that he was well regarded by his co-workers and employers.

When a neighbor encountered a period of unemployment that stretched over several months, grandfather intervened on his behalf and recommended his friend for a position at the Packers. Soon thereafter, a matter of weeks, the neighbor was promoted to the position of foreman — my grandfather's boss.

The man was embarrassed, not enough to refuse the position, but embarrassed enough that he apologized to my grandfather, admitting that he was certain that it was racial prejudice that prevented my grandfather from advancing at the plant.

My grandfather, stung and humiliated by the rebuff, resigned from Canada Packers. His former employers were as surprised by his expectation to be given a position of authority over White men as he was by their bigotry.

His self-esteem was further tested when he could find no other work than shining shoes in a barber shop. He had been a man who had always believed that all honest work held its own dignity and he tried to apply his beliefs to his life then, but could not.

The forties were ending, most of his children had embarked upon their own lives, it seemed to be the right time to make a change in his own. The railroad companies in Winnipeg were fast becoming the largest employers of Black men in Western Canada and soon enough my grandfather found himself among them.

It did not seem, to my grandfather, or to other Black workers of that time, that the railroad was just another ghetto for Black labourers. The rail companies provided stability, travel benefits and more money than most of them could have hoped to earn elsewhere.

The CPR, although seen as daring by some for hiring Blacks at all, did not adopt its policy to satisfy purely altruistic motives. They actively discriminated against Whites when hiring, because Black men were willing to work for less money. They continued to reserve positions of authority for Whites and they enforced a policy that restricted Blacks from handling the baggage of White passengers.

In 1942, when both the CNR and the CPR were enacting legislation to restrict Blacks to "porters only" status, A. Phillip Randolph, president of the Brotherhood of Sleeping Car Porters, arrived in Montreal to organize Black railroad workers in Canada into a union, which after some years of negotiations with both railways, achieved full promotional rights for Blacks and wage parity with Whites in other occupations.

Eventually, when conditions for workers on the railroads were much improved and wages became attractive to Whites, the railroads abandoned their policy of non-White hiring. Fortunately for the Black families who depended upon these jobs, the new policy did not entail firings or layoffs. Gradually, however, through attrition and a shift in the attitude of young Black men toward working on the railroad, fewer Blacks were seen in the once Black-dominated brotherhood.

My mother and Pearl declined to go to Winnipeg with their parents and their two younger brothers, Bert and David, who were still in school. Pearl had found a job that she enjoyed at the Army and Navy in Regina; my mother was looking for work, confident that a good position would be offered to her in the short term. At that time, Regina high schools helped to place graduating students into the work force, the system being that those students achieving the highest overall average would be placed first.

My mother stood by, frustrated, watching classmate after classmate find employment, until she and only a few remained jobless, despite her finish very near the top of her class.

One of her teachers, troubled, called her in for a talk. He was very sad, but there was nothing that he could do, he told her. None of the hiring companies, including the government, would accept her.

While my mother was experiencing daily battles to become employed, her oldest sister Ethel was experiencing the end of a most unsuitable marriage. Aunt Ethel was taking her leave of Calgary, partly to escape the possibility of interaction with her ex-husband and partly because, as the newly single mother of a small daughter, she needed the emotional support of her own mother.

The two of them, my mother and her sister, departed for Winnipeg together.

In the very beginning, Winnipeg appeared to be welcoming. My grandfather had found immediate employment with the CPR and the job's stability, wage and their savings permitted my grandparents to make a down payment on a small bungalow.

However, my Uncle Bert has told me, before there was time for them to take a breath in their new home, a threatening note appeared in their mailbox. They were not welcome in the neighborhood, the note said, among other equally disturbing things. Claiming to be representative of the community, the note was unsigned. My grandparents, very distressed, decided to attempt to discern the source and truth of the letter.

Grandfather knocked on every door on either side of the Smith bungalow, covering the entire length of the street. No resident that he spoke to claimed knowledge of any kind regarding the letter that he held in his hand. Some of the neighbors, appalled by the note's contents, accompanied my grandfather as he covered the area. Finding no clue to the note's authorship on Ross Avenue, the group crossed the alley behind my grandparent's home, eventually ending the mystery at the house of an old man who lived alone and admitted to delivering the invective.

I do not know the exchange of words that transpired on the old man's doorstep, or if any of the neighborhood people spoke up. I do know that at the end of the incident, when they were all returning to their homes, someone assured my grandfather that the man was "a crackpot" and in no way represented the pulse of the community. My grandparents laughed together later in their home, remarking that the incident had been an effective, if somewhat unusual way of acquainting themselves with the neighbors all at once.

Meanwhile, my mother had made an appointment with a stenographic job placement agency.

After submitting to their mandatory typing and shorthand tests, she was shown into a small room equipped with a desk, occupied by a man who ceased shuffling papers and smiled when he saw her.

"We don't have anything for you right at the moment," he said, as she was halfway seated in the chair that she had been offered. "We'll be in touch as soon as . . ."

My mother interrupted. "I was told when I called," she said, still stinging from numerous employer's rebuffs in Regina, "I was told that there were several positions available immediately."

His smile faded a little. "Those positions are of a very high level. For advanced stenographers. If your typing was sixty-five words per minute or more, it would be different."

It was clear that he had not opened my mother's file, which was sitting in front of him.

"I type eighty words per minute," she said.

"We require short . . ."

She interrupted once more. "Look at my test results," she said shortly, then tagged on, "Please." Her interviewer checked her shorthand score, saw that it, too, was unusually high and blushed deeply. He barely raised his eyes, repeating the words that my mother did not wish to hear.

"We simply do not have anything for you right now, Miss."

My mother was angry, but helpless. Human rights commissions and fair-hiring legislation were yet to be invented.

Extremely disheartened, she vented her bitterness in a letter to Pearl.

She received a prompt reply from her twin, containing a message from her boss at the Regina Army and Navy. If my mother would be willing to return to Regina, he would be pleased to find a position for her in the A & N's secretarial pool.

Gladly, my mother followed up on his suggestion. She had missed Pearl, missed the familiarity of her home city and found herself back in Regina only weeks after believing that she had made her permanent departure.

She thrived at the Army and Navy, advancing very quickly to the position of private secretary to her beloved Mr. Williams, who seems to have been an unusual man for his time, completely blind to racial barriers.

Not long after my mother's return to Saskatchewan, Tommy Douglas' CCF assumed the provincial government and enacted legislation to protect minorities from racism in the job market, but my mother's Mr. John Williams practised affirmative action before it was required of him by law. He was very deeply interested in my mother's life and they retained their friendship long after my mother got married and moved away, until Mr. Williams' fatal car accident in 1955.

Summer in Winnipeg

*When she's Black, she's very,very Black
and when she's not, she isn't . . .*

*B*etween Regina and Winnipeg, I read and reread *Black Beauty,* tormenting my family with enthusiastic talk of hairstyles that I might try or cosmetics that I might send away for. Long after the others had lost interest and fallen asleep I harangued my faithful sister Noël, who, not yet having reached the age where she was interested in beauty, Black or otherwise, nodded politely when I whispered, "I think this style would look good on you," and pointed to a model on a page.

Winnipeg was experiencing a hot, dry spell when we arrived, perfect weather for my brother and our cousin Lorrie (for Laurence Jr.) to throw a baseball back and forth between them or take the younger boys to the river in search of frogs. My sister, who had been patiently waiting months for me to emerge from the fog that had enveloped me since my encounter with Brian, finally gave up and decided that if she was going to enjoy her vacation she would have to team with the boys. She left me to drift about Aunt Ethel's house on my own, usually reading in the basement or occasionally flopping on the couch in the living room, the better to hear what my mother and her sister were saying.

One day I found them listening to country gospel records.

"Don't you like Black gospel?" I asked Aunt Ethel. "Don't you like Mahalia?"

My aunt looked at my mother and raised an eyebrow.

"She's in a Black phase," my mother said in response to her sister's glance. "She doesn't like listening to this White people's music."

The two of them laughed. "Reminds me of my daughter," Aunt Ethel said. "When she's Black she's very, very Black and when she's not, she isn't."

Annoyed by what I perceived to be their cavalier attitude toward the problems inherent to Black youth, I rose from the couch and stomped down the hallway to Elaine's (Elaine being the daughter that Aunt Ethel had referred to) room, which my sister and I were sharing for the duration of our visit.

Although Elaine, who was ten years older than I, had long ago moved into an apartment, the bedroom had been maintained exactly as it was when Elaine had inhabited it and was still referred to as "Elaine's room."

I bounced angrily onto the bed and stretched out, staring up at the ceiling. I was convinced that my mother and aunt were mocking a conversation that Noël, Elaine and I had had the evening prior. I had explained to Elaine that I was no longer interested in pursuing relationships with White males following my negative experience with Brian at school, but my decision had narrowed the field of potential dates to negligible numbers.

"Any Black guys that I know are cousins of one sort or another, or I've known them since we were in diapers and it feels like we're cousins. I'm so tired of being the only brown face everywhere I go." My list of complaints was endless and Elaine, who, like Sharon, did not seem to take issue with our age difference, was very sympathetic.

"You want to know what's worse?" she had asked. "Try looking like me. People don't realize that I'm Black, so they never watch their mouths in my presence the way they would for you girls. You have no idea how racist people really are, how often they use words like 'nigger,' the things they say about Blacks and other minorities."

How often had I heard one relative or another say "Poor Elaine. She's so fair?" Elaine was fair, green-eyed and slightly red-haired.

"If a White man asks me out," Elaine continued, "I'm never sure if he knows I'm Black. What am I supposed to do, ask him outright?"

"It must be awful," my sister interjected.

Elaine nodded. "Wait until you get older, go to university or start working. You'll meet the few available Black men that aren't relatives and discover that they're only interested in dating White women."

"Sometimes I wish I lived in the States," I said. "At least I wouldn't have to walk around in a sea of White faces there."

It was at that point that Noël, Elaine and I realized that our mothers were eavesdropping. We heard them giggle from the kitchen, so outrageous did it strike them that a child of theirs would fantasize about living elsewhere than Canada.

I continued to lie atop my borrowed bed, suddenly feeling more drowsy than angry. I began to think ahead to the weekend, when Elaine would not be working. Noël and I would transfer our suitcases to her apartment, where the three of us would make popcorn and talk late into the night, in privacy.

I must have slept a long while. When I woke, Aunt Ethel was bending over me, about to cover me with a blanket. She had closed the window.

"What happened to the sun?" I asked.

"It's really clouded over," she said. "Those other kids will be back from the beach soon. What shall I make for supper?"

"Pizza," I said yawning.

She laughed. Pizza had not yet found its way into the Smith repertoire of supper foods.

My aunt sat down on the end of the bed and I shifted my feet to make room for her. We looked at one another.

"You know," she began slowly, "we know what you kids are going through. Don't think your Mama and I were laughing because we don't care about your problems."

"Why were you laughing then?"

She thought for a moment. "Because it makes us nervous to hear our children talking about the same things that we talked about when we were girls, the same troubles."

I sat up. "Did you not like to date White men either?"

"We never had the chance to find out whether we liked it or not. White fellows didn't date Black girls as a rule."

"That can't be true," I said. "Four of your five brothers married White women."

"I didn't say White girls didn't date Black boys, I said White boys didn't date Black girls."

"What's the difference?"

"The difference is that women don't care so much what color a man is. Men are different. When a man chooses a girlfriend he's concerned about what people are going to think of his choice, how she's going to improve his status."

"So you didn't date White men?"

"No."

"Did Aunt Edie?"

"No."

"Mom and Aunt Pearl?

"No."

"None of you were ever asked for a date by a White man?"

"Well, I think there were one or two fellows who may have been willing to give it a go, but they weren't fellows that we wanted to date."

"Why not?"

"They weren't from the church. Mama and Daddy wouldn't have approved."

"Because they weren't from the church?"

"Partly."

"Partly?"

"They didn't approve of us dating Whites."

"I don't believe you." I knew that my grandparents loved their White daughters-in-law, that they loved the children of those biracial marriages as much as they loved me and I pointed this out to Aunt Ethel.

"You know what your grandmother said to Sidney when he first brought a White girlfriend home and said he was thinking about marrying her?"

I shook my head.

"She said, 'Well, you better get you a paintbrush and some black paint then.'"

I was silent.

"They don't care anymore, but it took time and events to change your grandparents."

"What happened to change them?"

"Oh, I think it was partly my first marriage. I married the first Black man that I met that wasn't a relative and believe me that was after many years of staring out the window crying from loneliness while my White girlfriends were out having fun. He was so far from being right for me that he might just as well have been from another planet. After that disaster I think Mama and Daddy were more concerned about quality than color."

I returned to the original issue. "So it wasn't just that White men wouldn't date you, you were worried about your parents' opinion too."

"Yes, we were, but don't think I'm exaggerating when I say that there were very few White men who were willing to date outside of their race. It's changing now. Society is a bit more relaxed and there are lots of White fellows who will want to date you girls."

"I'm going to find a Black man who's so dark, so blue-black that White women won't want him," I said forcefully.

"Honey," my aunt said, shaking her head. "You've had a bad experience, but you'll get over it. When you decide to get married, you'll have your choice of all kinds of men, Black or White, and it won't matter."

"I won't marry a White man," I said. "I'll stare out the window and cry every night for the rest of my life before I'll marry a White man."

"We'll see," she said, standing up. "Meantime I'm going to make supper and if you'll help me it'll make you a better wife to whomever."

I ignored this last remark, which I knew was directed at my also recently blossoming feminist leanings. But I did get up and help.

The Bermudians

. . . it is no longer accepted outright that new generations of people will choose partners from the same racial background.

*M*y Aunt Ethel was speaking the virtual truth when she told me that she had married the first Black non-relative she met that was of her general age group. They moved to Calgary from Regina early in their marriage. Around the time that Elaine was born, my mother and Aunt Edie joined Ethel in Calgary for a variety of reasons. Ethel needed to work and it was agreed that my mother could live with her and her husband while taking her grade eleven at Western Canada High School, and watch Elaine in the early afternoon and evening. Edith, I believe, had come to think of Regina as a city that was very limited in terms of employment and social contacts for a Black woman of her age. There was no one for her to date, never mind to marry.

When compared to Regina's tiny Black community, Calgary's population of two or three hundred Black people seemed large and thriving to my mother and her two older sisters.

Edith, who was twenty-four years old, proved to be immediately popular with the local young men. She accepted a job as a cook at one of the vogueish Black-owned businesses, "The Chicken Fry," and news of her legendary cooking ability spread very quickly.

She possessed the classic characteristics that were desirable in a wife in 1946 — she was sweet, "good," attractive and classy and, as a consequence, was fervently pursued by single men young and old.

Many of her suitors were nice people who treated her respectfully, but none of them were "in the church" and therefore, none of them were acceptable. She was waiting for someone who, like herself, was a committed Christian and did not gamble, party, smoke or drink.

When she and my mother heard that a Black minister from northern Alberta was holding special services in downtown Calgary, they, like most Black Calgarians, decided to attend.

Andrew Risby was tall, strong and well-built, but to my aunt, more impressive than these surface attractions was his message. He was clearly a man of conviction, not some amorous hothead who prayed on Sunday and played on Monday.

The two of them became acquainted over the duration of the meetings and began to discuss marriage short months after they had met. My mother offered her enthusiastic blessing to the match between her cherished older sister and the dedicated young preacher.

Often, even now, inhabitants of the Black community will arrange meetings between young Black people of opposing gender. Someone's cousin will hear that a friend's nephew will be visiting from somewhere and there will be a surreptitious plan for the unattached niece to meet the fellow, whose parents are convinced that "deep down" he would like to meet a really nice Black woman.

This is done subtly because it is no longer accepted outright that new generations of people will choose partners from the same racial background. This is perhaps less true of Whites, who still comprise the bulk of Canadian society, but parents of marriage-aged minority children all face the "specter" of biracial dating in their families.

It is certainly true in the Black community today where, in Western Canada, we make up less than one percent of the population. Black parents whose children find Black partners are an anomaly.

In the fifties, when my mother and her twin Pearl began to cast an eye around for men, years after their two older sisters had been married (and in the case of Ethel, divorced) Black women were still most commonly looking for Black men and in Regina, looking to no avail. Subtlety was not called for when two Bermudian Bible students arrived in Estevan, Saskatchewan. The news quickly slithered through the community and as quickly as my mother and Pearl heard about the two men, the men heard of the twins and a meeting was arranged.

The foursome's early encounters were infested with peculiarities, beginning on the first date when Gilbert (my aunt's fellow) and Roy (my father) appeared, one wearing the jacket and the other wearing the pants belonging to the same suit, continuing with an incident on a bus where the two gentlemen neglected to pay their dates' fares (a major gaffe in 1952), and ending on a roller coaster at the Regina exhibition. Apparently, Pearl had persuaded Gilbert, who had never seen or ridden a similar contraption, to board the ride. Gilbert screamed in real terror as they shot down the first steep incline, reportedly shouting, "Pray, Pearl, pray! (He pronounced it "Peril") Pray that we get off alive and I'll never do anything so foolish again as long as I live!"

My aunt was mortified and that was her final outing with the shaken Gilbert Leigh. My mother had, in fact, all along been more forgiving of the two Bermudians' (Gilbert, I learned many years later, was in fact from Jamaica, but my mother had always lumped him together with my father as a Bermudian for conveniance sake) foibles, believing that these minor quirks would be ironed out once they had learned "the Canadian way of doing things." She mar-

Pauline's wedding day, Regina, August 1953.

ried my father in the end, of course.

Pearl, however, who had always been the feistiest of the four Smith sisters (to this day she remains the only one of them who has bothered learning how to drive) was determined to wait for someone who would not pray while riding a roller coaster, someone who was more than just appropriately Black, someone who was her all-consuming passion. She found him, a good number of lonely years later, hitting a home run at a baseball game in Calgary. She married Allen Hayes in 1956.

On the Banks of
the Saskatchewan River

Choices that had been made well before
I was born were affecting me now . . .

That summer in Winnipeg, 1970, actually was a small family reunion of sorts, partly planned and partly coincidence. My mother, sensing that her older children were less and less interested in making the two day (my father was . . . is, a very slow driver) drive across the prairies, wanted to make our vacation as special as possible. She knew that my grandmother's brother would be visiting from California and arranged our holiday to overlap his, so that we could meet our great-uncle.

Aunt Pearl and Uncle Allen decided that they, too, would travel to Winnipeg during our visit, along with their children Paula, Craig and Patti-Jo, who were close in age to my three younger siblings. With the addition of my cousin Joni (Olie's daughter) from Vancouver, who being close to my age was invited to keep me company, and my grandmother's cousin and grandniece from Oklahoma, the homes of my mother's Winnipeg family were soon to become very crowded.

My mother and Aunt Ethel had decided together, because my grandmother had recently been ill, that until the American visitors arrived, the rest of us would spread ourselves between her (Ethel's) home, Elaine's apartment, and Uncle Bert and Aunt Margaret's house, leaving my grandmother to conserve her strength for the coming onslaught.

I was not pleased by this arrangement. I had looked forward to long, quiet talks with my grandparents and felt cheated that I had travelled the long distance only to be denied the opportunity. Finally, growing weary of my sulking at Aunt Ethel's house, my mother agreed to let me spend two nights prior to the arrival of the other relatives at my grandparents' new home on Bartlett Avenue, extracting a promise that I not "get on the nerves" of my grandmother.

My grandparents were, of course, delighted to receive me. They found nothing moody or amiss in my behaviour, whereas I had begun to hear the others wonder aloud about the "healthiness" of a fourteen-year-old girl who preferred to stay behind and read books while her cousins and siblings visited the beach. My grandparents accepted my quietness as a natural extension of what they had always perceived to be my bookish nature. This was refreshing and relaxing for me.

We passed our two days together eating, napping and playing scrabble, a game at which my grandmother was a formidable opponent. My grandfather did not play. He lurked about us, his hands in the pockets of his grey, baggy pants, torn between his pride in me for being "smart" and his pride in my grandmother who, despite her limited formal education, played the game with a good deal of skill.

I had no trouble adjusting to this, their new home, although I was visiting them for the first time there. The house was substantially larger and somewhat newer than what they had left on Ross Avenue, but not so new as to make them seem out of place there.

It had a large tree in the front yard and a dining room to which one gained entry through a heavy, dark-wood archway, and a bright, warm kitchen with a floor that squeaked in a comforting manner.

It is impossible, now, to think of my grandmother without wanting to use superlatives to describe her — but there are no words. She was funny, practical and real. She made her grandchildren feel special and at times when we were far from her presence, just the knowledge of her love was enough to help you.

She and I had always talked easily. We talked together those two evenings. She was not an old woman; I was not a tremulous adolescent. We were simply people talking.

I had grown curious about my mother's life as a young woman, had begun to see my family as a group of people with a shared history that bore a great deal of influence on the life that I was leading. Choices that had been made well before I was born were affecting me now.

Because I was not certain of exactly what I was trying to ascertain, I questioned my grandmother about seemingly inane topics — what had she worn to my mother's wedding? What did she eat for supper when she was a child?

She did not turn my questions aside and gradually they became more reasonable.

"Why did you come to Canada?" I asked her.

"My father brought me," she said. "We travelled most of the way by train, then by ox cart."

"Did you want to come?"

"My mother didn't want to come. I was nine years old and wanted her to be happy, so I felt sorry."

My grandmother's mother, Katie Manning, had met my great-grandfather, Willie Glover, and married him in Oklahoma (probably at Chandler, as that is where my grandmother was born and she was their first child).

They came to Canada in 1912 and, as my grandmother told me, made the last part of their journey to their homestead at Turtleford County, Saskatchewan, by cart. They had to ford the river at one point and my great-grandfather chose a spot where the water was low. My grandmother and her numerous young brothers and sisters looked over the wagon's edge at the brown water sloshing about the wheels. The oxen strained as the wagon began to slow, then finally came to a stop when its wheels were deeply buried in the mud. My great-grandfather, along with his wife and my grandmother in their skirts, disembarked to push and pull with the beasts. They managed to free the cart and reach the shore, mud caked to their legs and clothing.

This harsh introduction to life in Canada did not endear the country to Katie. She never grew fond of life in the Saskatchewan wilderness and for years implored her husband to return her to Oklahoma and the family that she loved. He refused to do so, curiously, until after she died, at which time he returned to America, where he remarried and added one son to his family, the very Howard Glover, in fact, who was expected in Winnipeg imminently and who our mother had brought us there to meet.

My grandmother never spoke disparagingly of her father. She had long ago forgiven him for his autocratic parenting style and any heartache that he had caused her mother, and had taken him into her home for his last years.

He lived until I was ten years old. I knew him simply as a gentle old man until he died at the age of ninety of complications from a gangrenous leg that had been amputated.

Family legend has it that his trouble with the leg began one day when he was chopping crops in a field. He is said to have accidentally hacked the large toe of one of his feet halfway off. Deciding that the toe was of no use hanging in that manner, he sliced it off completely with his machete and tossed it over his shoulder into the field behind him.

Later that evening, my grandmother showed me a photograph of herself, taken when she was barely sixteen years old. She had the photo done to send to my grandfather, her fiancé who had departed "overseas" during the First World War.

She was wearing a white dress and had her hair pulled back with a white flower, a gardenia perhaps, next to her right temple. Her face bore an odd expression. Only her eyes were smiling, her mouth was almost pouting. It was as though they had a secret, or a joke and she had put the expression on to remind him of it.

On the back of the photograph she had written, "To George Smith, compliment (sic) of Arrenna Glover." That was all. Nothing about loving him or the marriage that they hoped to embark upon if he returned safely.

Grandfather during the war, circa 1918.

The first time my grandfather saw my grandmother she was thirteen years old. They, along with one hundred or more of the Black settlers who lived around Maid stone, Saskatchewan, had gathered to help one of their neighbors in some task of his farm possibly to raise a barn and, of course, to socialize. It was probably in the late fall, after the crops were in but before the snow came to force them into isolation from all but their nearest neighbors.

My grandmother laughed when the men rose to attend to the work and my grandfather joined them, taking his hat. "He thinks he's a grown man," she whispered to her mother.

She helped to prepare the meal that, upon the return of the men, all the people gathered around the large tables to eat.

It was 1915. Many of the Black pioneers had now been in Canada for five years, some for longer than that, and they had grown accustomed to this way of helping, of leaning heavily upon one another to survive in the strange climate of the country that was less than the promised land they had hoped for.

After joining hands and singing" grace," they began to laugh and talk and eat the abundance: the ham, chicken, roast beef and gravy, the greens, potatoes, peas, carrots, the corn bread and the fresh, warm bread covered in butter that someone had just pulled from the oven.

My grandparents were just two very young people that day. They did not know that four years later, after the war, they would stand together on the banks of the Saskatchewan River, in Turtleford County, and be married there with these same friends and relatives for witnesses.

They did not know, of course, that they would be married for sixty years and raise nine children, or that, fifty-four years later, she would sit with her granddaughter in a Winnipeg house and remember that day, the day that they met.

Belonging

. . . racism is not your responsibility,
it is the responsibility of its perpetrators . . .

I returned to Calgary from Winnipeg not with my family in our old car, but with my Aunt Pearl, Uncle Allen, cousins Paula, Craig and Patti-Jo, the new baby.

Before my mother and Pearl had children, they had agreed to help one another raise them. Pearl's first child, Daryl, died at three months. Following his death she relied heavily upon my mother's calm for her next two children. Paula and Craig stayed with us while my aunt worked until they reached school age. Aunt Pearl promised that she would take her turn when my mother's children reached adolescence.

I confess now that when I was fourteen and in subsequent years, I made her repay the debt many times over. My gregarious aunt empathized with youthful disturbances, seeming young and close to her own girlhood. She was attractive and wore trendy glasses with rhinestones embedded in the frames.

I enthusiastically accepted her offer of a return ride to Calgary, settling into their Lincoln knowing that, with my uncle driving, the journey would take less than a day.

Sitting in the front seat, I held the small, beautiful Patti on my lap as she slept.

"Did you like Howard?" I asked Aunt Pearl, referring to the great-uncle that I had met in Winnipeg.

"Oh yes, yes I like him. He was good to me when I lived in the States," she said. "Did you like him?"

"At first I was a little . . . I don't know. I thought he'd be older. And more like Grandma."

She laughed. "You won't meet a whole lot of people like your grandmother, honey."

We rode along in silence. By then we had been travelling for some hours and the dusk was advancing. Uncle Allen reached for the headlight switch.

"I didn't know that you lived in the States," I said.

"It wasn't for long." My aunt was yawning. "I stayed with Aunt Grace in California before I got married. Al and I had had a fight and I wasn't sure if I wanted to marry him. When I visited Howard in Los Angeles, he showed me the city. He took me to Disneyland but it wasn't much then. Not much more than the Stampede." She yawned again. "Anyway, he knew that I was from the church and respected that, didn't take me anywhere wild, though I'm sure that Howard is on good terms with all the wild places."

"Did you meet guys?"

"Uhmm hmm. That's why I went, to see if there was anyone more reasonable than the big guy here."

"That was crazy," I said.

"You tell her, kid," Uncle Allen interjected.

Aunt Pearl laughed. "Well, reasonable or not, after three months away I knew that I loved Allen Hayes and the only thing to do was to come back and marry him."

We grew silent once more. I was quite certain that, if I got married, my husband and I would be like them, Aunt Pearl and Uncle Allen. We would be able to casually say that we loved one another, we would hold hands even when our children were teens. My husband might address me by an affectionate nickname, the way my uncle sometimes called her "Poil."

It was by now quite dark. My aunt had fallen asleep, her head slumped to one side. The small cousin to whom I had been administering a bottle of milk slept in my arms. Paula and Craig, curled up in the back seat also slept.

I said, "Everyone is tired," to my uncle to let him know that I was vigilantly awake, that I would keep him company.

"They sure are," he replied.

We sped along, the pavement visible only as far as the head-lamps beamed, the tall grass and scattered trees along the Sas-katchewan highway now swallowed by the night.

Calgary . . . I was going home, where I would have a few weeks remaining of summer, then yet another year at Bowness High School. Another year of my life.

But it would be different. I would be fifteen, stronger and clearer than I had been before.

I was growing toward a quiet confidence that I could not yet articulate, even in my thoughts. I had learned more about my family's history, about what it meant to be Black in North America, about my own blackness in eight months than what I had cared to know all the previous years of my life. I was beginning to under-stand that I had the right to exist in my world.

This may not be comprehensible to someone who has not lived as a peculiarity, the idea that a child must one day tell herself, "I am allowed, I was meant to be, I have the right to exist." But when you are a Black child who looks out into the world and sees hostility toward Blackness, you begin to ask why, you look for rationality behind hostility, until the day you realize that racism is not your responsibility, it is the responsibility of its perpetrators. That day, you say, "I belong in the world. I belong here in Western Canada where my family has lived and worked for four genera-tions."

We drove on, the miles peeled away. Back to Calgary and my life there.

*I*t was by now very late in the summer, the prettiest time of year when every day was hot and green and I suffered from my usual pre-September melancholy. There was nothing left to do. I had my new clothes and books, I had called Clem and Laura to let them know that I was back. We had ridden our bikes around lazily, but it seemed pointless to engage in strenuous activity so close to the school year beginning.

I was very relieved when I woke up one morning and learned that Uncle Dave and Aunt Barbara were in Calgary and Aunt Edie had invited us all to dinner. It meant that I would see my Vancouver cousins — Rick, Brenda and Janice — and that I would consume yet another legendary feast prepared by Aunt Edie.

The Risby's had recently moved into a newer, much larger home, equipped with two kitchens. That day, as I wandered toward the upstairs kitchen I could hear the visiting Aunt Barbara talking to her sister-in-law, my Aunt Edie. They were speaking in hushed tones, having one of the adult conversations that I always liked to get in on.

When they saw me, they stopped talking. I asked if I could help.

"We're nearly ready, honey, just waiting for Andrew."

Uncle Andrew was at the table, tossing a salad in an enormous bowl.

"Hello," I said to him.

"Hi, Mustard Girl," he said in the high voice that he reserved for all children under the age of thirty. "Mustard Girl" is what he had called me when I was younger and had demanded that mustard be spread over any food that I consumed.

Aunt Edie said again that things were ready and that I should go ask my mother to say the grace.

The house seemed to be filled with a hundred people, all talking at once. On the way to find my mother I grabbed the arm of my youngest brother as he was racing past, pulled him to me and squeezed him.

Uncle Dave, who was watching, called out, "Big sister likes ya', hey Dee!" My brother, "Didi" we called him, grunted, looked down at his shoes and wiggled away from me.

After my mother's prayer, which was always longer when there was company, we formed a snaky line and began to wind our way around the oval table, stacking our plates to their very limits.

We engaged in a fairly typical Edie Risby banquet. In addition to the tossed salad, we chose from bowls of mashed potatoes and gravy, sweet potatoes, spinach with bacon, buttered corn and peas, cauliflower with cheese sauce, cabbage rolls, sugared ham, turkey, dressing, fried chicken, roast beef and sweet, warm, home-made rolls.

Minutes after we had gorged on the main courses the table was covered with pies — apple, raisin, peach, pumpkin, banana cream, lemon meringue and raspberry — and cakes — chocolate, angel food, white chiffon and coconut. Nothing else that I might have been doing could have made me happier that day. I ate banana cream pie and chocolate cake and was offered coffee, which pleased me even though I did not like coffee.

I was with my family, we were safe, the world was out there, my Uncle Dave was grinning at me from across the room.

"Don't be in a hurry to grow up," he had said to me when we passed at the table a few moments earlier.

"What do you mean?"

"How old are you?"

"Almost fifteen."

"You see?"

"Okay," I said, mimicking the adults in the family, who said "okay" frequently.

"You know your old uncle loves ya', eh?"

He had an unusual way of speaking out of the side of his mouth, sounding mumbly and slightly nasal.

I pursed my lips as though I had to think first, and then nodded.

Desolation

Our progress was very slow,
I had time to look ahead and behind . . .

Early in 1976, I went to the Holy Cross Hospital to see Sharon. I went in the evening, with Richard, and for some reason, I don't know why, I wore a new sweater and makeup, as though I thought she would know me and comment upon how well the colors I wore suited me.

As the result of an accident, she had lain in a coma for more than two months, but I had chosen to stay away. I waited and waited for someone to call to say that she was fine, that she was sitting up and talking. The call did not come, day after day passed, until finally I gathered the courage to see her.

She looked far worse than I had imagined.

Richard and I stood two feet from the bed, saying nothing for ten minutes. At last, my head and hands trembling, my throat so tight that I could hardly breathe, I stepped closer and choked out her name.

"It's me, Cheri," I said. "Do you understand me?"

She began to move her arms and her head.

I could hear Richard's breathing.

"It's almost as though she can hear you," he said.

I called her again and she began to moan.

Richard hurriedly left the room.

When he returned, a nurse was with him and they walked very quickly.

"It seems like she's responding," he was saying, "like she's trying to say something."

"Sharon," I said again.

Her eyes passed vacantly across the ceiling, then back.

The nurse took Sharon's hand and bent down near her ear.

"Sharon," she said loudly, "we want you to talk. Can you squeeze my hand?"

She waited, then straightened and shook her head. "I'm sorry. We look for something more definite. We look for a controlled action of the hand or a word or the eyes to focus. I'm sorry."

The nurse left us.

We left the room and walked to the elevator, rode it to the ground floor and hurried through the corridor. I thought of a time, not long before, when Sharon and I had been in that same hospital together, visiting her boyfriend, a football player, who had taken a hard hit in a game.

"I hate hospitals, man," Sharon had said in this same corridor. "I hate the smell."

We reached the parking lot and Richard led me to his car.

I thought of her alone in that room, with the eerie little light over her bed, hearing the sounds of the machines that were keeping her alive and the detached voices of dispatchers over the intercom.

Two weeks later, when someone telephoned to say that she was dead, I was watching an old film on a small black and white television in my room. I switched it off and sat on my bed.

I was nineteen. I felt such desolation that I cannot explain.

The procession of cars leading to the cemetery where Sharon was to be buried was the longest I had ever seen. Our progress was very slow, I had time to look ahead and behind at the unbroken line of vehicles. I looked out, also, at the people who did not know

Sharon, people who were going shopping and to other appoint-
ments, who would be late because they had to wait for our caravan
to pass.

My family has developed a curious mechanism for dealing
with loss, which was more apparent than ever when we were all
together for Sharon's funeral. It is nervous laughter that often
evolves directly into sobs.

We were at the Risbys' house the day after the funeral — my
mother's siblings and their spouses, Sharon's brothers and sister,
my family, Great-uncle Chester and Great-aunt Drucilla.

Poor Aunt Drucilla. She had always been a very beautiful
woman, petite and quite delightful in a scary, eccentric way. (When
I was young and on a visit to her farm near Edmonton, I had grown
bored and asked to have the television turned on. Aunt Drucilla
said, "That's the devil's box. Only Uncle Chester watches the
devil's box in our house." I was about eight years old and wasn't
sure if she was serious. We locked eyes for a few seconds, then
she chuckled and gave me some kool-aid, but she never did turn
on the television.)

She was afflicted with Alzheimer's, which we called senility
then, in her sixties. At the time of Sharon's funeral she was still
functioning, a sweet person, but confused. She was very interested
in all of us and our lives, we were her brother's children and
grandchildren, and she loved us.

She had been particularly fond of Aunt Edie and Uncle
Andrew's children and had known them quite well while they were
growing up, so it was a surprise when she turned to Beverly and
said, "Honey, don't you have a sister? I don't see her here. Where
is she?" Her eyes scanned our faces, looking for Sharon among us.
Beverly was taken aback by the question and opened her mouth to
speak but didn't know what to say.

Uncle Chester, who was sitting beside his wife, took her hand
and intervened. "Remember baby?" he said in a soft voice. "We're
here for the funeral. Her sister's gone on to be with the Lord."

Aunt Drucilla turned back to Beverly with real sorrow in her
eyes. "Your sister's passed on, honey?"

It was a terrible evening, achingly real and surreal all at once.

Sometimes people were laughing at silly things, sometimes people cried suddenly, sometimes we sat through long, silent stretches.

Later, I was alone in my room. I had one photograph and a stack of music that she had introduced me to. From the stack I selected my most worn album, "What's goin' on?" by Marvin Gaye. One song, "Wholly Holy," recalled to me one of her apartments, a night years before when I had been stretched out on the floor in the dark living room, listening to the music while she puttered in the kitchen.

On the edge of my bed, I sat and ran my hands across the fringes that hung down. I wondered what my life would be like now that she was no longer in it.

Things would happen to me and she would not hear of them. I would live, make friends, have children that she would never know.

Discoveries

. . . she had walked, talked and breathed as a Black woman . . .

$\mathcal{A}$ few months after the funeral I flew to Winnipeg to see my grandparents. In a way that seemed connected to Sharon's death, or not wanting her to be dead, I had developed a preoccupation with our family and its ancestral history. Perhaps it was more a preoccupation with mortality. My grandparents were elderly and would die, possibly sooner than later. The loss of them would leave me with unanswered questions.

They were, of course, delighted to see me. Grandma's hair was thin, she was thin and seemed weak, but Grandpa was robust.

I did not tell them that I had come for a specific reason. I had no desire to barrage them with questions or communicate my fear that they would die.

Instead, we talked quietly after a scrabble game in the bright kitchen in the afternoons, or over a late evening snack in the dining room that was always called "lunch," and if I found an opportunity I would urge them to tell me something about their lives.

It was in this way that I made two discoveries.

I learned of a persistent but unproven family rumor that my grandfather's mother was White, and I learned that my grandfather's father was a slave.

Somewhere inside I must have known that I was a descendant of American slaves, but I had never acknowledged it. My own great-grandfather was a slave and I had not known, perhaps had not wanted to know.

As for the rumor concerning my grandfather's mother, I had only to look at him to see that it was possibly true.

It was my grandmother who let slip this bit of news, but I addressed my questions on the matter to my grandfather, as it was his mother that we were discussing.

He had said nothing, had not even looked up when my grandmother said, "Some are telling it that George's mother was actually a White woman."

When I asked my grandfather if it was true, he shook his head. "Some believe it. I don't believe it," he said.

"But who says this, who started this rumor who released this information?" I persisted.

My grandfather shrugged, obviously disturbed by the conversation. I waited until finally he spoke again. "Mama is said to have told Hub and Sis (referring to his brother Herbert and sister Bertha) when she was dying." He shook his head again. "Why would she tell only them and none of the rest of us? 'Ya' take, a man can look at his own mother and know what she is."

I looked very hard at him. If it were not for his hair and the fact that I knew he had lived his life proudly Black, he could have been White, and had in fact been mistaken for White on numerous occasions by people who were judging him physically (and with a hat on).

My grandfather did not wish to believe that his mother had lived a lie for most of her life, that she had walked, talked and breathed as a Black woman, only to reveal upon her deathbed that she was, in fact, not Black. I understood his reticence and did not press him.

(This matter is still vigorously debated among my family. As a young woman, my great-grandmother was described as "beautiful, with long, flaming red hair and grey eyes." Others add, "Yes, and her hair had a crimpy wave and her lips were full." There are those who believe it and those who don't.)

Over the remaining days of my visit, I received no more information about his mother from my grandfather and only scant details surrounding his father's life as a slave. I left Winnipeg with a number of questions which rested for many months.

The Rumble of Wagons

. . . sometimes a person will choose their race,
rather than being born to it . . .

*B*y the time I reached my early twenties, I no longer regarded Aunt Daisy with fear, or even awe. She was a tiny, sweet, bird of a person, the only surviving sister of my grandfather to whom I still had access. (His other living sister, Drucilla, their mother's namesake, you may recall, had been debilitated by Alzheimer's.)

Daisy and I had developed a kind of symbiotic relationship; she possessed a formidable memory and had written four hundred pages of script pertaining to our family's history. Finding in me someone who was eager to read the notes and ask questions, we spent a good number of hours in one another's company, sometimes alongside a tape recorder to which she had no objection.

In the way of many of my family's members, she thoroughly enjoyed the role of story teller. When she described a character she made them live. When she remembered the Saskatchewan River that rolled through the countryside near her father's homestead, I saw its banks, crowded with poplars that reached out over the water. I heard the rush and lap of the water beneath the shouts of the semi-naked Black children of the settlement who fished and hung from the trees.

It was she who supplied the details that I had been missing from my great-grandparents' lives, which I now intend to relate as they were told to me.

In the early nineteenth century, an African named Kudjo lived near the Nile River in Ethiopia with his wife and three children.

One morning while going about some task of his everyday life, the African observed from a safe distance some White men who were removing various and sundry items from a rather large ship. He watched them for some time, then returned to his wife and told her what he had seen.

Curiosity compelled him, over the next few days, to repeatedly return to the site where the ship was harboured.

Gradually shedding his initial apprehension of the White men, he approached and was immediately befriended by them. They offered him gifts for himself and his family, which he accepted.

Following some weeks of daily discourse, the ship's captain urged Kudjo to attend a party that was to be held on board the ship that evening, and to bring his family. Kudjo's wife, who had become alarmed by her husband's casual disportment with strangers, refused to go along to the party, refused to send her children, and begged her husband to reconsider attending.

The African ignored his wife's warnings, went to the party and drank himself into a state of unconsciousness.

When he awoke, he was far from his home and the family that he would never see again.

In America, the enslaved Kudjo ran away repeatedly until he was given a wife, with whom he produced three new children. One of those children, a male called Jackson, was born on July 14, 1822.

According to the story as Aunt Daisy told it, Kudjo began to run away again after the birth of his third child, saying only that he wished to be free.

Asleep in the branches of a tree one evening during his final attempted escape, he was awakened by the barking of hunting dogs that had tracked him there. Shot at close range, he crashed to the earth, dead.

I know nothing more of the fate of Kudjo's American family, except that, as a young man, Jackson was purchased by an Arkansan plantation owner named "Captain Smith."

Jackson Smith returned to the Little Rock county plantation along with the Captain, who explained along the way that he had purchased the young slave as a husband for his daughter, Mary.

I would imagine that Jackson Smith was more than minimally surprised to learn that his new owner was also to be his father-in-law.

Captain Smith, who appears to have been an unusual southern slave-owner, lived with his half-Black mistress and their daughter, who was Mary, in an impressive mansion on his land.

When Mary was twelve years old, her father suddenly and inexplicably announced plans to marry a White woman, displacing Mary's mother from her privileged position as woman of the house. Shortly after this tumultuous event, Mary's mother became ill and died. (Of heartbreak, according to Aunt Daisy.)

It is then reported that Captain Smith and his new wife produced a family of unknown proportions, and that these children loved and fully accepted their older half-sister Mary.

It was when Mary was nineteen years old that her father embarked on the journey that culminated in the procurement of Jackson, the son of Kudjo, for her husband.

A small, comfortable cabin was built for the young couple on the Captain's land. They had three sons, two years apart; the first was Tommy, the second, my great-grandfather, Rufus Sadler (born July 10th 1856, one hundred years before me) and finally, William, who they called Billy.

Jackson Smith was made overseer of the plantation, and his three sons, to his joy, were given what was termed "freeborn" status. Never knowing what it was to be slaves, the three boys enjoyed an education, the run of their grandfather's land and the deep affection of the people around them.

The circumstances of these people's lives were odd, even bizarre.

With the onset of the Civil War in 1861, life on the Smith plantation grew ever stranger, with Captain Smith aligning himself to the South and Jackson Smith joining the Northerners as a Union soldier.

I have been unable to gain any information that would illuminate how this split affected the relationship of the two men, who up to this point had obviously shared a close and trusting bond. One can only imagine the number of ways that the Civil War impacted on the daily operations of the of the Smith plantation.

Mary Smith, partly Black herself had married a Black man and had borne his Black children. Her father, her brothers and her sisters were White southerners. After 1861, she must have found it increasingly difficult to live between the two worlds.

While the Captain and Jackson Smith were away, engaged in the war, the women that they had left realized that they were vulnerable to attacks from marauding bands of "bushwhackers." Mary's younger half-sister, fearing that some harm could come to my great-grandfather and his brothers, interrupted their school lessons one day to take them for a walk among the rose bushes that lined their property. She led them to a small opening in the vegetation through which there was room for them to squeeze and not be easily seen from the path. She informed them that they were to go directly there if they heard any unusual noise or wagons while they were playing.

Sometime in 1862, Captain Smith was injured and returned to his Arkansas home to recuperate.

While strolling through his orchards early one evening, he heard what he thought, correctly, was the rumble of several wagons coming toward him on the path. With some difficulty, attributable to his age and his wound, he climbed into one of his trees to await the wagons and discern the purpose of their visit.

Unknown to him, a scout on foot had been sent ahead of the wagons and had seen the Captain's hiding place. This spotter shot Captain Smith, then continued his silent approach toward the houses.

Minutes later, the man who had murdered her father burst into Mary Smith's home, where she was eating the evening meal with her sons. Holding a gun to her head, he and his companions bound the three children and ransacked the cabin. Then, kicking and screaming, my great-grandfather and his brothers were dragged to the wagons and tossed in among several other small Black boys.

The last thing that Tommy, Rufus and Billy Smith saw was their mother lying face down in the dust, sobbing, and their aunt, their tutor, sprinting along after them, shouting to the pitiless kidnapppers that these little boys were not slaves.

A week later, the body of Captain Smith was found hanging over the limb of a pear tree when his family saw buzzards circling overhead.

The three young boys with whom we are concerned travelled for weeks in the wagons. My great-grandfather described to Daisy and she to me, how they lost track of time and how they slept on the splintered wood of the wagon floor. He said that Tommy, who was eight years old, wept continually and told their captors that their grandfather was a very important man who would expend every effort to find them.

In 1862, trading in slaves was illegal in Arkansas and a number of other states. For this reason, the wagoneers proceeded to Texas, where the slave market was yet thriving.

Tommy was sold very quickly, but before Rufus and Billy had taken their places on the auction block, he was brought back and instructed, very roughly, to stand quietly beside them.

"What happened?" my great-grandfather whispered to his brother.

"Quiet Ruf," Tommy said. "I told the man who bought me that we were stolen and he said he didn't want no trouble. He brought me back and I think those men will have to take us home now."

Three days later, the brothers were still travelling in the wagons, which were by now nearly empty, as most of their companions had been sold.

At some point on the third day, the carts halted and one of the abductors told Tommy that he was going with him to water the horses. Tommy obeyed, leaving their wagon with a pail in each hand. One of the men walked behind him through a field of tall grass.

Not long after Tommy disappeared from their sight, Rufus and Billy heard a gunshot and they never saw their brother again.

For the next six years of his life, my great-grandfather lived and worked on a small farm owned by a man whom he was instructed to call "Master Ed." At the hands of these three people, the farmer, his wife and the farm cook, Rufus Smith suffered more misery than he could ever have imagined.

When he was twelve years old, he decided to run away. He was young and completely unaware that, in fact, he was already "free," that slavery had been outlawed less than a year after his arrival on Master Ed's farm. He filled his pockets with onions and stole away before dawn one morning, accompanied by the farm dog, who was the only friend that he had known there.

Rufus had a vague plan that he would return to Arkansas, but not knowing where that was, he wandered along unfamiliar roads for days, until he began to grow very weary of eating onions.

He came to a farmhouse where, standing in the field next to the house was a team of horses, hitched to a plow but lacking a driver.

The door of the house stood open. Receiving no reply to several knocks, Rufus stepped inside and shouted, "Somebody here?"

In the room just beyond the one that he had entered, he could see a table spread with foods of the sort that he had not tasted since he had been taken from his mother.

Nervously, he sat down to eat, fearing what the occupants of the house would do if they returned to find a ragged Black stranger feasting at their table.

Rufus and his dog ate all that they could. He then stuffed his pockets and resumed his journey, still directionless but considerably less hungry.

For six years, my great-grandfather meandered from town to town and farm to farm, working for food, clothing, or the promise of pay that never materialized.

In 1874, when he was eighteen years old and spurred by what circumstances I do not know, Rufus Sadler Smith arrived in Little Rock, Arkansas. One could scarcely describe the delight that my diminutive great-aunt took in relating the story of her father's reunion with his family.

Her ability to manipulate language and to create verbal tapestries was uncanny. The quality of her voice was smooth and soft, but not false.

Rather than simply saying, "Father walked all the way to Arkansas from Texas," she would say, "Papa travelled on, walkin' in that heat and the dust until the shoes was just rags on his feet."

She would draw the word "rags" out for several beats and then cut off sharply on the word "feet." In this way, after seeing the overworked leather of the shoes, it was very easy to see the rest of the man: his utilitarian, ill-fitting clothing, his stride, the hat that he might lift to wipe his forehead, the expression that would have come over his face after hearing a stream from which he could drink.

She would retell an encounter so that you could see the speakers and know just how black that man's face was and how he scratched the stubble on his chin as he spoke.

My great-grandfather found that Little Rock had changed enough to be unrecognizable to him. He walked up one street and down another until he saw a Black man riding a mule.

"Beg pardon," he called out.

The man halted his beast and turned to Rufus.

"Yes?"

"Do you know anything about the Smith plantation? My grandfather has a farm somewhere nearabouts."

"Why, yes," the Black man said. "I know them people well. Are you one of Jackson Smith's boys, one of them three little boys that got stole away?"

"Yes, Jackson Smith is my father," Rufus told him.

The stranger and his mule carried my great-grandfather to his parents' home, telling him along the way that his grandfather had been killed the same day that Rufus and his brothers had been kidnappped, and that his mother was in poor health.

"Mary has been quite poorly of late," he said when they had come close enough to see the house. "You best slip off here and walk now. I'll ride up ahead and prepare her you're coming."

George Smith, Rufus Sadler Smith and Drucilla Smith.

My great-grandfather learned from his parents that there had been no word from Billy, and they from him that Tommy was dead. He then settled into a farming life near them, eventually meeting and marrying Drucilla Threat.

There are two sidebars to this story that I must now relate, as they illustrate a curious factor that I have discovered about race, that being that sometimes a person will choose their race, rather than being born to it, and occasionally society, or fate, if you like will decide a person's race.

Jackson and Mary Smith had been given an orphaned male, White child to raise shortly after their own sons were stolen. The child, named Will Curtis, lived among Black people and considered himself to be no different from them. Naturally enough, when the young man fell in love, it was with a Black girl, whom I understand to have been very dark. He wanted to marry her, but was strongly discouraged from doing so by the people he had always known as his family. Jackson and Mary Smith, and my great-grandfather Rufus, told him that he should look for someone of his own race. Will moved to a town in a nearby county and met Drucilla Threat, who like himself, appeared to be White but believed herself to be Black. He was again cautioned by his family not to marry her. "The difference," they said to him, "is that you look White and are White. She look White, but ain't."

Deeply confused and saddened, I am sure, Will Curtis went to live in the Ozark Mountains and married a "hillbilly" girl.

My great-grandfather's motive for discouraging his stepbrother in his pursuit of Drucilla must be called into question, for it was he, of course, who married the pulchritudinous Drucilla in the end.

The ultimate irony of the story was revealed in the deathbed confession reportedly made by Drucilla to her daughter and son.

She had been raised by a former slave and midwife in Alabama, a woman known to everyone as "Grandma Ann." Although Drucilla was fair and red-haired and her sisters and brother were dark, she never questioned the story that she looked the way she did because her father had been a White man.

When she was twelve years old, Drucilla was sent to Arkansas to live with her Aunt Rose, never knowing the reason until 1908, when she, by now married and the mother of twelve children, returned to Alabama to see her original family.

At that time she learned that she had been born illegitimately into a wealthy White family. Grandma Ann, who had overseen the child's entrance into the world, was asked to take the child and never to reveal her identity.

When Drucilla was twelve years old, her adoptive mother learned that two of the child's natural aunts were preparing a plan for her future that involved removing her from the custody of Grandma Ann.

Before these women had time to activate their plan, Drucilla was transported to Arkansas where she lived with Grandma Ann's sister until she married my great-grandfather.

It was this secret that she guarded for forty years, that, upon its revelation brought upheaval to future generations of Smiths, and that caused my grandfather, in 1977, to stare out the window at his back yard and hum.

Pin Cherries
and Other Berries

. . . he was a kind of Moses, leading his family to the promised land . . .

On April 16th, 1912, my great-aunt Daisy celebrated her fifth birthday at a tiny train station in a town called Delmenie, Saskatchewan.

That day, she said, it was "pourin' down rain. It was pourin' down rain when we pulled out of the station in Oklahoma and it was pourin' down rain when we pulled into Delmenie, Saskatchewan."

She had been travelling with two older sisters and two older brothers, and the five of them were greeted by their mother and eldest sisters, Maude and Mary. They walked to a house that someone in town had rented, and as Daisy dashed from beneath the protection of their umbrellas to pick flowers that she saw growing along the path, her mother despaired, calling out to the little girl that she would "catch her death."

It had been more than two years from the time that my great-grandfather Rufus had announced that the family would leave Oklahoma to live in Canada, and almost two years since the family had been together. Rufus had arrived in Saskatchewan in 1910, along with hundreds of Black American farmers, mostly Oklahomans. He, like his fellow immigrants was given a parcel of land, 160 acres, for the filing fee of ten dollars. He built a cabin and began to make preparations for the arrival of his wife and twelve children, who would come in twos and threes until the summer of 1912. Then, they would begin to live in their new world, as Canadians.

Grandfather and Buster (Rufus) seated.

My great-grandfather transplanted his family approximately ten times in the waning years of the nineteenth and early years of the twentieth centuries. He was restless — nervous about the welfare of his children living Black in an increasingly hostile society. Especially after his parents' deaths (Jackson Smith on December 12, 1892 and Mary Smith on March 7, 1893) he no longer felt tied to his birth state, Arkansas. He, along with multitudes of former slaves, drifted into two districts known then as "Indian Territory" and "Western Territory," lands that, although within the boundaries of the United States of America, were not states. Black people could vote in the territories.

This attempt to remain a step ahead of total denial of human rights was only a mediocre success for Rufus Smith and his peers. Blacks could vote in the territories, but they were not welcome there. Lynchings and houseburnings were as common in the territories as elsewhere, but Black people, cornered, believing that they must seize their humanity in the territories or be crushed, fought their enemies with every means available to them. Black men, including my great-grandfather, joined the Socialist Party of America, which at first promised to uphold them. The Socialist option proved to be a disappointment for Blacks when the party, reluctant to alienate poor White farmers and labourers, began to renege on its early commitment to Black concerns.

Frequent armed encounters between Blacks and Whites prompted Rufus Smith to move from town to town in the Indian Territory — from Wagoner to Bristow, to Fischer and finally to Tulsa, where the Smith family settled into a white house with a fence, on Frankfurt Avenue. This is where they were living in 1910 when Blacks lost voting privileges, three years after the territories had been merged into a state called Oklahoma.

At precisely the same time the Black Oklahomans were being brutalized by southern law, the Canadian government was taking out full-page ads in southern newspapers, offering 160 acres of land in its unsettled western provinces to anyone who could produce the filing fee of ten dollars.

To the almost unanimously Christian Blacks, the juxtaposition-ing of these two events seemed to be much more than coincidence. Many of them began to believe that the "Promised Land" for which they had been searching throughout their lives lay to the North — a country about which most of them knew nothing except that it had sheltered weary slave travellers at the end of their journey on the underground railroad.

Along with the loss of his voting rights, two other events propelled my great-grandfather toward changing his descendants' history forever by making us Canadians. One was the death of his younger brother, Billy.

Rufus and Billy had regained one another through a bizarre happenstance of events in 1902. While sitting at the ringside of a circus with some of his children, Rufus was startled when one of the circus performers passed close by him and called out, "Hello Bill!" Believing it to be a simple coincidence, he said nothing. When the stranger passed by again, however, looked directly at him and shouted, "Bill," once more, Rufus could think nothing but that the man with the dog act had mistaken him for his younger brother.

When the circus had finished, he approached the man and learned that indeed, he had known a man in Texas named Bill Smith who bore a strong resemblance to Rufus. My great-grandfather acquired an address and sent a letter immediately, to which he received a quick reply. Billy was alive, married with children, and had lived all along in Texas from the time that he had been sold as a four-year-old boy into slavery. The brothers established a bond and visited one another frequently until Billy, who had never enjoyed perfect health, died at the of 51 on October 31, 1909.

Following Billy's death, Rufus Smith had no further family or emotional ties to the South. He had already begun formulating his plan to leave Oklahoma when, early in 1910, something happened to speed his preparations along.

One day, Rufus's son-in-law, Ben Howard (married to the second daughter, Maude) who was employed at a cotton mill, asked my grandfather, George, if he would like to accompany him to work that day.

My grandfather, pleased and excited by this acknowledgement of his maturity, put on a new suit of clothes and promised his sister Maude that he would listen to Ben and not get in the way.

Unfortunately, there was a palpable tension between Ben Howard and his foreman, a man by the name of Garfield, which reached an apex that particular day when Garfield weighed Ben Howard's load of cotton.

Howard pointed out that he thought there had been a mistake, that his load was undervalued. Garfield took umbrage at what he thought was an accusation of cheating and the two men began to argue bitterly.

My grandfather, who was our family's only witness to the event, said that only after Garfield attacked his uncle with a weapon (I am unsure of what the weapon was) did Ben Howard pull his and fire.

He pushed my grandfather out of the way of the dead man's falling body and my grandfather, uninjured, stared down at his blood-spattered suit.

Ben Howard and my grandfather boarded the wagon and rode back toward Tulsa in silence, but before they reached the town a neighbor came riding on his horse to meet them.

"Someone's been to town from the mill, Ben," he said. "The Sheriff is coming for you. You'd best get away and I'll take the boy back with me."

My grandfather climbed down from the wagon and onto the back of the neighbor's horse. Ben Howard wheeled around and made for the Canadian border, with the clothes that he was wearing and the money in his pocket.

I have tried to discern why, as Ben Howard shot a man in self-defense, he was afraid to return to Tulsa. Perhaps if Garfield, who was a married man with five children, was White, Howard's reluctance could be easily explained. Clearly, for whatever reasons, Ben Howard was not willing to face a trial in Oklahoma.

He changed his name to Jim Mack and established himself as the foreman of a Saskatchewan lumber mill before sending for his wife, Maude, and their two small children.

In a matter of months, the rest of the Smith family began their transfer to Canada.

Ben Howard, or Jim Mack as he was now known, lived the rest of his life terrified that American law enforcement would find him. He and a number of other family members blamed the bad luck that plagued him in Canada, including the accidental death of his little son, Leon, on the "karma" of what had happened at the cotton mill.

On January 25, 1924, he was run over and killed by a bus on the corner of Albert and DewDnee Streets in Regina.

It is known that, a week or two before he died, two "Redjackets" (this is what my ancestors called Mounties) appeared at the Mack household door, inquiring after the whereabouts of "Ben Howard."

I have heard speculation from more than one family source that Jim Mack/Ben Howard may have stepped purposely in front of the Regina bus, fearing that after fourteen years of hiding in Canada, the law was about to pounce on him.

Some residual innocence, or naivete from my childhood, allowed me to achieve adulthood with my belief in Canada as a non-racist society intact. I had experienced racism of the individual variety, but I trusted that my country's history was unblemished by sweeping, legislated bigotry.

Only when curiosity about my family's place in the Canadian demography prompted me to read about the reception of Blacks into Canada, only after I dissected my own family's oral histories, did I recognize my error.

Canada has frequently practised discrimination based on color and race, and every recognizable minority that lives here today has felt it.

The prospect of "too many" brown, black or yellow people making their home in Canada has, in the past, filled many White Canadians with fear, and in some cases, loathing. The same is true today.

When my great-grandfather crossed the forty-ninth parallel, he believed, in the way that many Black people of his time drew Biblical analogies to their own lives, that he was a kind of Moses, leading his family to the promised land. He had heard the Canadian winters could be harsh, but, having nothing in his past to teach him the meaning to the word "harsh," he was unprepared. He was also unprepared for Canadian racism. He learned that Canada's message of welcome had not been intended for him, or others like him.

We, the undersigned residents of the city of Edmonton, respectfully urge upon your attention and upon that of the government of which you are the head, the serious menace to the future welfare of a large portion of Western Canada, by reason of the alarming influx of Negro settlers. This influx commenced about four years ago in a very small way, only four or five families coming in the first season, followed by thirty or forty families the next year. Last year several hundred Negroes arrived in Edmonton and settled in surrounding territory. Already this season nearly three hundred have arrived; and the statement is made, both by these arrivals and by the press dispatches, that these are but the advance guard of hosts to follow. We submit that the advent of such Negroes as are now here was most unfortunate for the country, and that further arrivals in large numbers would be disastrous. We cannot allow as any factors the argument that these people may be good farmers or good citizens. It is a matter of common knowledge that it has been proved in the United States that Negroes and Whites cannot live in proximity without the occurrence of revolting lawlessness and the development of bitter race hatred, and that the most serious question facing the United States today is the Negro problem . . . There is not reason to believe that we have here a higher order of civilization, or that the introduction of a Negro problem here would have different results. We therefore respectfully urge that such steps immediately be taken by the government of Canada as will prevent any further immigration of Negroes into Western Canada.

This petition, issued by the Edmonton Board of Trade and supported by the signatures of 3000 Edmontonians, was typical of reactions to Black immigration into Calgary, Winnipeg and Saskatoon. Also typical were threats of violence (which, true to gentle Canadian nature, were mostly not acted upon) and newspaper editorials carrying headings like, "DARK INVASION" and "NO DARK SPOTS IN ALBERTA."

Canada's Liberal government, whose intent in advertising for pioneers throughout America had not been to attract Black farmers, faced the wrath of Canadian citizens and the Conservative opposition in the House of Commons. One such Conservative member is known to have stood one day to enquire whether it would not be wiser to ". . . preserve for the sons of Canada the lands they propose to give to niggers."

The dilemma of the government was this: how to squelch the flow of Blacks into Western Canada without interfering with the campaign to attract White farmers?

Attempts to censor inquiries from American farmers that arrived through the mail were pointless, as no envelope gave any clue to the color of its sender. Endeavors to find Blacks unfit to enter the country were ineffective also. Most of the Blacks that possessed the courage to migrate to an unknown land were also in excellent physical and financial condition. Bribing the border doctors was futile, as too few of them were willing to accept money to falsify records.

The solution that worked in the end was simple. The Canadian government hired a few Black men to travel throughout the American Southwest, to warn Black churches and organizations about the horrors of life in Canada. These paid men convinced thousands of Black people that Canada was barren and frigid, and offered them no better opportunities than what they already had.

Black immigration into Western Canada slowed, then trickled, then stopped in 1912, four years after it had begun with its "four or five families coming in the first season."

For the approximately two thousand Blacks who had already settled in Alberta and Saskatchewan, these developments were disappointing. Their numbers would remain small. It had been their hope to build an independent community that existed peacefully alongside its neighbors. They now believed that it would be a struggle for their community just to survive, let alone to be an example of Black success and racial harmony to the rest of the world.

Worse than this was the unsettling awareness that their welcome to Canada was not what they had expected, that their quest for a racial nirvana had been naive.

There were two benefits that my great-grandfather and his peers reaped from their lack of large numbers in Canada. One was a network of closeness and support for one another. The other was that the Klu Klux Klan seemed to be unaware of their presence.

When the original furor over their arrival had subsided, the prairies' Black settlers analyzed their circumstances and most of them concluded that they had done the best thing for themselves and their families. Canada offered Blacks the right to vote, unsegregated education for their children and a relatively peaceful existence alongside their White neighbors, whose attitudes ranged from sullen tolerance to unfettered acceptance. Their lives were unmarred by lynchings and cross burnings.

My own family, the Smiths, formed many strong friendships with their White neighbors, in particular a young English couple named Jenny and Charlie Body and another family called Hill. In 1918 when my great-aunt Bessie turned sixteen years old she aroused the ire of her father by eloping with David Mayes, a lad from the Eldon District. The newlyweds curtained themselves at both the Hills' and the Bodys' until they were discovered by Rufus. He packed his daughter off to Maidstone in his wagon, where he forced her to wait outside, shivering, while he filed a complaint of kidnapping against her new husband. This incident, which would have been quite comic had it not entailed gun-toting and seriously wounded feelings, was happily resolved in the end, after involving nearly every Black family north of Battleford. David and Bessie Mayes carried on with their marriage. (It is said, by the way, that Bessie, who weighed ninety pounds on her wedding day, eventually required two scales to weigh herself.)

It is also clear, however, that Rufus Smith did suffer, if not from racism itself, then the fear of racism.

During his first winter in Canada, my great-grandfather, knowing that he would need a full team of horses in the spring, mortgaged the three that he had brought with him from Oklahoma in order to buy another. The children soon came to know this new horse as "mean ol' Barney." One day, while in the act of kicking at eight-year-old David with his hind legs, "Barney" fell over, dead.

Rufus had planned to pay for Barney with the profits from his first crop. Instead, having no means to work his farm and no available funds, he was forced to relinquish his three good horses to Barney's original owner, at the hands of a Mountie. Rufus explained that the horse had died before he'd ever been put to use, that he must have been sick before he was sold, but the "redjacket" was adamant. My great-grandfather believed that he had been victimized, but he had heard that his new community looked unfavorably upon Black immigrant farmers with complaints against White men. He said nothing as he watched his three horses, and only means of support, being led away.

Losing the horses was the first in a series of blows that hobbled the Smith family's attempt to settle smoothly in their new country.

In February of 1915, Tommy Smith died, the victim of an ailment which seems to have been exacerbated by northern Saskatchewan's unkind winters. (I have never been able to identify his illness, but surviving Smiths say only that Tommy was "not right" from birth.

Later that year, on the first day of school, tragedy again struck, in the form of a bizarre wagon accident that fatally injured Leon, the six-year-old son of Maude and her husband Jim Mack.

Life seemed rather grim to my great-grandparents, especially when they considered Rufus' advancing age. He was now sixty. In part to ease their parents' need, my grandfather, George, and his brother Herbert accepted employment as farm hands on a settlement near Lashburn, sending by mail to Rufus and Drucilla most of their monthly wage.

In addition, my grandfather and his older brother, John, bought their father a team of oxen who bore the monikers "Pete" and "Red" and enabled Rufus Smith to begin farming his land once more.

When I consider my family's early history in Canada, the year of "Pete" and "Red," 1916 is my favourite year.

Not only did the addition of the ox team return the Smiths to a state of healthy well-being, it allowed Rufus the money and resources to complete the new log house, which he had been building in stages for five years.

This cabin had two bedrooms upstairs and one off of the kitchen which was occupied by the young David and his brothers when they visited home. In the evening, David was likely to warm himself at the black stove that sprawled across the kitchen, then carrying the heat with him, he would dash for his bed in the next room.

David and his sisters appreciated the luxury of real wood beneath their feet, rather than the sod floors that they had endured in the interim cabin.

The children, who had at first found the heavily treed countryside around them dense and claustrophobic (different as it was from the sandy and red-clay terrain they had left in Oklahoma), now began to appreciate the woods, especially when the summer brought an explosion of fragrance, color and fat berries.

Rufus had bought new horses with the first of Pete and Red's profits, which the Smith children sometimes rode to nearby lakes, or, more often, the Saskatchewan River. Although few Smiths, even today, are good swimmers, that generation did enjoy fishing and rafting on the boughs of trees that they strapped together.

There were two good crops that year, one on Rufus' homestead and one on the section that son John had abandoned after realizing that he preferred expensive clothing and Saskatoon's relative sophistication to life on the farm. The family now raised hogs and kept a few cows, from whose milk Drucilla and her daughters churned butter to sell, along with eggs and the wheat from Rufus's crop.

More than once Aunt Daisy recalled for me in detail how happy they were that autumn as they prepared for the winter ahead. She would hold her hands up in front of my face, so that I could imagine how black they became after two hours of pulling vegetables from her mother's garden. There were turnips, carrots, beets, potatoes and cabbage, which her mother transformed into a huge barrel of sauerkraut and stored in the cellar.

Some of the eggs, she preserved, some of the cream she churned into butter and with the last load of wheat she filled the house with loaves of baked bread.

After school, the children were sent with buckets into the woods, to collect a variety of berries. Drucilla would can or make jam from the saskatoons, raspberries, strawberries, gooseberries, pin cherries and other berries that the children gathered.

"When everything else was ready," Aunt Daisy said when she spoke to me of this happiness, "Papa slaughtered two of the hogs. Us children felt like we were ready. Ol' winter could just come on and he wasn't going to bother us none."

She rested her head back, paused, closed her eyes. She was recalling herself and her family as they had been in their contentment in 1916 -- loved, sheltered and well fed.

The year 1916 is tangible, as though it was a part of my own history and memory. The autumn time — for communion with neighbors, baseball, feasts, barn-raisings — was the bridge between summer and winter, work and survival, and my forbears walked and lived.

My great-grandfather persevered through ten more Canadian winters. I have not heard anyone say that he ever thought of leaving.

He died in Regina General Hospital on April 14th, 1926. Throughout their lives together, he had referred to his wife as "Julia" and she had called him "Mr. Smith." No one who is alive today can tell me why they did so, yet I cherish this unexplained bit of knowledge for its quirkiness. Two people who called one another by names that no one understood, who lived before me and were happy in 1916.